The Process Prescription

How Your Business Can Improve Results, Reduce Risk, and Grow Faster

Mark Spencer Palmer

1423
Interests

1423 Interests LLC
Dallas, Texas USA

Thanks to those who reviewed early versions: Bronwyn, Cayce, Declan, Kenny, Jennifer, Jesse, Lang, Mariam, Richard, Sarah, and Sisi.

Some names in the text have been changed to preserve anonymity.

Published by 1423 Interests LLC
www.1423interests.com

Library of Congress Classification: HD62.12
Dewey Decimal Classification: 658.022
Print ISBN: 979-8-98-815688-8
Ebook ISBN: 979-8-98-815689-5

First edition

Table of Contents

Chapter 1

The Benefits of the Process Prescription

A process story: Lemonade

I hate buying insurance. Or at least "strongly dislike" since my mom taught me it was impolite to say "hate." What other product do you pay a lot for, then hope you never use?

Homeowners insurance, life insurance, title insurance, car insurance, health insurance... ugh.

I saw an ad for an insurance company named Lemonade. An odd name, but maybe they're playing off the expression, "When life gives you lemons..." So I give them points for effort. Intrigued, I went to their website to find their price for homeowners insurance. Thankfully, there were no photos of a fake family having fake fun in front of their fake house, which needs to be insured. Just a plain, easy-to-read page with a button labeled "Check Our Prices."

I clicked. A questionnaire asked me one simple question at a time, and I had a quote for homeowners insurance in a few minutes. Their price was better than my current policy and their deductible was lower as well. Had I found a winner? Or a fluke?

Lemonade's online reviews were strong. Their mobile app rated 4.9 out of 5.0 in the App Store, and they had a Financial Stability Rating of "A (Exceptional)" from Demotech, an insurance rating firm.[1]

I moved forward with the sign-up process. It took only 13 minutes from when I logged into their website until I received my policy via email. The policy information was in easy-to-understand, plain English.

A few days later, I had a question about my coverage, so I submitted an inquiry using their online form. While waiting for an answer, I decided to call them instead. I resolved things with a helpful person on the phone. The next day I received a call from the person who received my online question. She wanted to make sure everything was resolved to my satisfaction.

To be fair, I've not had to make a claim and I hope I never have to. But everything I've seen indicates that they process claims quickly. I still don't like insurance, but they made buying it less painful.

How did this happen? *Process success.* Lemonade developed and optimized several processes:

- How to develop a web page that focuses on what the customer wants
- How to provide a rapid, online quote
- How to route calls to knowledgeable people
- How to explain policy options and benefits concisely
- How to manage risk and keep premiums low

How can your organization achieve this kind of success?

The Process Prescription provides a step-by-step method for identifying your processes and making them better.

A process story: Rust

The actor Alec Baldwin stood in a wooden church building at Bonanza Creek Ranch, near Santa Fe, New Mexico. He was rehearsing a scene from *Rust*, a low-budget western film.

Baldwin was preparing to demonstrate how he would quick-draw and fire his gun for a scene. An assistant director handed him a gun and announced, "cold gun." On a movie set, this means that a gun is not loaded.

As Baldwin practiced the scene and faced the camera, he drew the gun, and it accidentally discharged. The bullet passed through the chest of Halyna Hutchins, the cinematographer, and lodged in the shoulder of director Joel Souza. A script supervisor ran outside the church and called 911. Ambulances arrived 22 minutes later, and then an emergency helicopter arrived. Hutchins was airlifted to the University of New Mexico Hospital in Albuquerque, where she was declared dead.[2]

How did this happen? *Process failure.* Multiple process failures. A live bullet had been loaded into the gun, violating safety protocol.

The crew failed to follow one or more of these processes that day:

- How to safely load a gun. This includes checking the rounds as they are loaded into the gun to ensure they are not live ammunition.
- How to keep people out of the firing line
- How to wear protective gear
- How to inspect the gun before use. This includes checking the gun barrel for obstructions and confirming that all bullets in the gun are dummy rounds or blanks.
- How to keep all live ammunition off the set
- How to secure and monitor the guns, blanks, and dummy rounds at all times

Jeff Harris, a plaintiff's attorney, said this to the Los Angeles Times about the shooting:

"The problem is when people get complacent and don't follow the systems, then that's when we have these accidents on movie sets. It's just unfortunate that we have to have these kinds of things occur before people really say, 'You know what, we've got to follow these written policies and we have to do it to a T. Otherwise, one mistake, somebody dies.'"[3]

If a process goes wrong in your organization, it may not result in death. But there are situations in plenty of industries where someone could get hurt if a process fails. Some examples include construction, healthcare, food service, transportation, and legal defense.

If you work with chemicals or hazardous materials, you need written processes. Or if you work with children or vulnerable adults, you need written processes.

But even if a mistake does not result in tragedy, why make unforced errors? If you can prevent lost revenue, a damaged reputation, or unhappy people, why not do it?

As long as humans are involved, there will be accidents and mistakes. But is there a way to reduce the bad and increase the good? What's the solution?

The Process Prescription provides a solution. The Process Prescription helps you do things better and faster while minimizing the chance of doing wrong things.

What is a process, and why should you care?

A process is the sequence of steps that someone or something follows to do useful work.

A process is a recipe you follow to get the result you want. If you're an elementary school principal, you have a process for how to conduct a fire drill. If you're a manufacturer, you have a process for how to buy raw materials. If you're a plaintiff's attorney, you have a process for how to prepare for a trial.

You have processes across all your organization's areas: hiring, training, customer service, development, facilities, management, and finances.

Your business functions as a complex organism with many inputs and outputs. Just like your body needs food, water, and oxygen—your organization has essential inputs such as people, suppliers, and technology. You succeed by enabling team members to run processes to deliver products and serve customers.

Your processes work together to help you achieve your organization's primary aim or mission.

This book will help you identify and refine the processes which convert your business inputs into valuable outputs.

What is the Process Prescription?

The Process Prescription is a step-by-step method for identifying and improving the processes in your organization.

When a doctor writes a prescription for you, you're expected follow some steps such as taking a pill or working with a therapist. In turn, you expect a result, such as a healthier body or less pain. Following the steps in the Process Prescription is a healthier business.

Figure 1-1. The Four Main Steps. Continue reading to gain ideas and methods for applying each of the four steps.

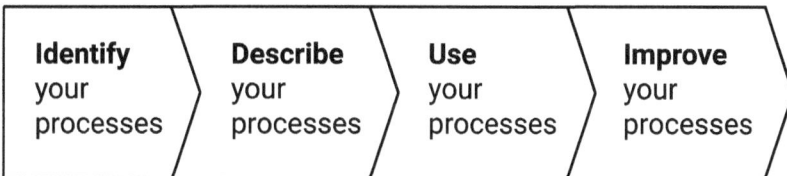

Identify your processes	**Describe** your processes	**Use** your processes	**Improve** your processes

We will cover each of these steps in detail in the coming chapters.

What you put into the Process Prescription is the time and effort it takes to follow the steps in this book. What you get out of the Process Prescription is a documented "business operating system" with a wide range of benefits.

What are the benefits of the Process Prescription?

The Process Prescription helps your business run on defined, repeatable processes instead of unwritten rules and memorized routines. Your business becomes more valuable and more sustainable. The Process Prescription provides a foundation that allows you to build a business that you want: one that requires less day-to-day involvement from you, one that is less stressful, one that is more profitable, or one that you can sell.

Even if your business will never be sold, the Process Prescription helps your next generation of leaders succeed.

Applying the Process Prescription allows you to strengthen your organization in several ways.

- Improve results. Move your business forward in a systematic way. Identify and emphasize your best processes. Eliminate bad processes and minimize waste. Do things faster. Improve the customer experience. Streamline existing processes to make things even easier.
- Reduce risk. Reduce the fragility that comes from depending on a few people who store key knowledge or information only in their heads. Prepare for a team member's departure. Reduce the damage from adverse events. Create a Plan B for each point of possible failure.
- Grow faster. Replicate your success. Get organized for growth. Increase clarity. Offer new services. Expand to new locations.

The Process Prescription for Startups

A startup company's needs differ from a more mature organization with existing processes. A startup needs to focus on the processes that meet customer needs and generate enough cash to survive. As a company grows out of the startup stage, it can add more processes to handle new opportunities.

A new company has the challenge of not only creating a valuable solution but also convincing customers to pay for that solution. This is referred to as finding product-market fit. A startup can apply the Process Prescription to refine processes for the following:

- How to assess customer needs
- How to identify a profitable niche
- How to test a product idea for product-market fit

- How to create a saleable product quickly
- How to find and build on sales success

Who benefits from the Process Prescription?

The Process Prescription is designed for business owners and leaders who are ready to improve how things work. Small business owners can apply the Process Prescription across their entire organization. Leaders in larger enterprises can apply the Process Prescription to their particular group or department.

I've seen the Process Prescription work in a various businesses: schools, non-profits, technology companies, service providers, and product companies. And I've seen the benefits from various perspectives I've held: owner, employee, consultant, adviser, volunteer, and board member.

The Process Prescription helps the people at all levels of your organization: executives, managers, and front-line workers. Also, everyone who interacts with your organization benefits.

To be clear: the Process Prescription is not to everyone's taste. The Process Prescription offers specific benefits, but it requires effort. For some people, the required change in culture and attitude is too much. Be honest with yourself.

A personal trainer can tell me to eat better and exercise more often. But if I don't act on that advice, I won't see the benefits. If I merely enjoy the *idea* of working out, but I'm not willing to get up, go to the gym, and exert myself, I won't get results. If I don't want to spend the time and money required, I won't get anything in return. Once I begin working out, I need to keep going.

You'll need to ask yourself if the Process Prescription is worth pursuing. The Process Prescription benefits leaders who are able to supply a few key ingredients.

Key Ingredient #1: You've identified a need

You should be able to identify something that could work better or something that's frustrating. You're not complaining, though. You see parts of your business that aren't running as smoothly as you'd like. You know that the whole business will run better if the parts run better.

The need for the Process Prescription stems from four types of problems.

- **Consistency problems.** Your team doesn't always know the best way to do something. This creates ambiguity and confusion.
- **Results problems.** You're not getting the exact outcomes you want.
- **People problems.** Your team gets frustrated and makes preventable mistakes. Or only one person knows how to run a process, and the process is not written down.
- **Timeliness problems.** Things are done too early, too late, too slowly, or not at all.

Process Needs Related to Consistency

Ambiguity: "Things are confusing or undocumented."

If you haven't written down how you do things, this leads to uncertainty about how things should be done. It also leads re-work and wasted time as you figure out how to solve the same problem again and again. For example, a non-profit has to file an annual report with the government. The form comes with lengthy instructions that need to be interpreted for the non-profit's particular situation. The form generates questions each year: Which responses can stay the same from last year? Where do I get the underlying data? Who should review and approve the form prior to submission? If each of these questions takes a few extra minutes to resolve because the answers are not written down, the filing process will take longer.

If you haven't written down how to do things, your team can be unsure about the best methods, who's responsible, and when things are due.

In contrast, the Process Prescription provides clarity. Each person has one or more defined roles. Each role owns a set of processes. Processes are scheduled as needed. Everyone gets a clear job description based on their assigned roles and processes.

Lack of Standards: "Things are done differently every time."

Even if things are getting done, are they done the best way every time?

Inconsistency appears along multiple dimensions. Time-related inconsistency means that sometimes things are done quickly and sometimes slowly. Sometimes things are early, and sometimes they're late. This variation makes it difficult to plan or set expectations. People-related inconsistency happens when one person does the same job much better (or much worse) than everyone else. Location-related inconsistency occurs when some locations achieve better results while others do much worse.

Removing these inconsistencies allows you to replicate your best work. You create valuable intellectual property that describes the methods you've developed. You can scale up your business since you've removed chance and randomness from the way things work.

Sloppiness: "Things are messy and disorganized."

Sloppiness is a drag on your business. Things take longer to find. Things stay dirty. Things get damaged. Things get lost. People can't take pride in their workspace.

In contrast to this, the Process Prescription keeps things neat and tidy. Collect and organize your key processes in one place. Create a Process Library that contains guides for organizing every aspect of your business.

Lack of visibility: "We don't know what's going on"

Can you see the processes that make your business work?

To understand what's happening, you need to visualize how things work. You need to see how your processes flow before improving them. Visualizing processes is more challenging for service-oriented and information-based businesses, but it's possible.

The Process Prescription provides transparency by creating a Process Library that describes all of your processes. You can then choose which areas need more attention as you work to solve problems, streamline operations, and improve results.

Process Needs Related to Results

Inaccuracy: "We make more mistakes than we want."

Errors cause problems. Defects need to be repaired, replaced, or redone. If an error affects a customer, they need to be talked through the fix or at least be notified.

In contrast to this, the Process Prescription systematically reduces errors by describing the right way to do things. Describe how to use the right tools with the right methods. Demonstrate how to check your work as you go. If an error does occur, you can make a note of what happened and why. Root out the underlying cause to further reduce the chance of the error occurring again.

Poor outcomes: "We're not getting the output we want."

If you're not getting your desired results or profitability, you need a way to find and analyze the underlying causes. Work on fixing the causes, both inside and outside your organization.

The Process Prescription provides a process-level view to see what's happening and improve results. Refine your systems faster by asking probing questions to pinpoint problems and opportunities.

Risk: "We're facing too much uncertainty."

Risks are all around us: we must live with the possibility of data breaches, regulatory infractions, supply disruptions, theft, and natural disasters.

Even if some risks are unavoidable, we need to take reasonable precautions to prevent losses. If something bad happens, you don't want to trigger a chain reaction that permanently damages your business.

The Process Prescription provides a systematic way to evaluate your risks. Rate each of your processes in terms of its risk factors, then decide how to mitigate these risks.

Process Needs Related to People

Unshared expertise: "Only one person knows how to do that."

Do you have valuable know-how held by only one group or person? If so, this is an information silo. Key data and experience are locked away and not shared with other departments or internal groups.

If useful information is not being shared, other groups have to waste time and effort figuring out how things should work.

Unshared expertise also poses a single point of failure. If something happens to that person, you would have to rebuild that knowledge from scratch.

In contrast, the Process Prescription describes roles, the related processes, and the knowledge linked to each of those processes. This permits collaboration, sharing, and improvement.

Lack of accountability: "We can't see who's done what and when."

Can you see what's been done and when? Do you get feedback on whether essential tasks have been completed? Is this confirmation solely up to the person doing the work, or are there other checks in place to make sure everything gets done on time? Even the most experienced and responsible person can sometimes forget, get distracted, or have an emergency that prevents them from completing a task. Nobody's perfect.

The Process Prescription provides a simple way to add accountability. You can set standards to make sure things are done the right way at the right time. See who needs to do what, by when, and how.

You can create a schedule and track task status and completion without repeatedly asking, "how's it going?" or "are you done yet?"

Unhappiness: "Our customers or team members are unhappy or stressed."

If your team members are unhappy, this spills over into other areas. They're less likely to stay. They're less likely to welcome and assist new team members. They're less likely to treat your customers well. This leads to unhappy customers.

The Process Prescription provides ways to measure and improve the satisfaction of your team and customers. For example, you can create a process to gather feedback in a consistent, repeatable way. Use this feedback to fix the problems you discover.

You can measure satisfaction over time to see if you're improving. Spot problems before they get too big. Find ways to serve your team and customers better. You'll experience less stress, more growth, and fewer surprises.

Process Needs Related to Timeliness

Lateness: "This wasn't done on time."

Are tasks being completed when they ought to be?

If things are getting done too slowly, it's helpful to identify the processes and sub-processes that are the largest contributors to the slowness. After pinpointing what's taking too long, you can alleviate the bottlenecks, speed up the essential steps, and eliminate unnecessary steps.

If things are late too often, dig into the underlying processes to figure out what "being on time" really means. Are you setting unrealistic expectations for due dates? Do you need to start working on a task earlier? Are there external dependencies beyond your control that slow things down? Are there internal constraints, such as competing priorities or a lack of tools?

The Process Prescription provides an organized way to identify your late processes and find patterns and solutions.

Omissions: "This wasn't done at all."

Are there things you should be doing but aren't?

If there are habits that would be helpful to acquire, take a systematic approach to instill and practice them.

An omission could be a small thing you keep forgetting to do, such as updating your website to remove old content or past events. Or the omission could be a bigger project that's hard to find time for, such as having an executive retreat to focus on strategy for the years ahead.

The Process Prescription provides a way to get a holistic view of everything your organization does, so it's easy to spot things that are missing. You can ask, "Am I spending enough time on strategy and planning? Am I tracking and analyzing my results? Are my competitors doing things that I should be doing, too?" You can assess the entire breadth of your organization's activities and find gaps that need to be filled.

American statesman John Adams said, "Every problem is an opportunity in disguise." Even as you uncover your organization's process imperfections, you are discovering untapped potential. You are finding new ways to make things simpler and new ways to make your customers happier. You'll find many ways to improve as you dig into your processes.

Key Ingredient #2: You're willing to do the work to improve

Those who succeed with the Process Prescription are willing to put in the work to get organized. They're willing to adopt a systems mindset and create a culture process improvement. A step-by-step approach like the Process Prescription requires time and patience. Each step is not difficult, but you'll need persistence.

You'll need to be willing to investigate how your organization functions and then capture your organization's valuable knowledge.

Your underlying motivation for doing this work can come from various sources: a desire for less stress, more growth, a stronger organization, happier people, or better financial results.

Whatever your starting motivation, you must allocate time to do the work. As the proverb says, "All hard work brings a profit, but mere talk leads only to poverty."[4]

The Process Prescription involves identifying and describing your processes. But this work shouldn't create frozen artifacts from "that process project" that came and went. You'll need to commit to continuous improvement in order to produce sustained results.

Consider a construction company that wants to improve its proposal submission process to prospective customers. Examining their existing process, they discover many variations: different proposal formats, multiple approvers, and multiple estimation methods. Everyone has a different idea about the best way to create a proposal. They might say, "It's too much work to standardize this. It's too complex. Forget it! Let each sales rep do their own thing... as long as the proposals get sent." This attitude misses an opportunity to filter out the noise and create a streamlined proposal process that everyone can use and improve. With the current system, proposal quality depends on the talent of each sales rep. Some proposals will be great, some will be so-so, and others will be lousy. What if everyone used the best process to create the most effective proposals? How much could the business benefit?

Just like with physical fitness, results come after putting in the work. If you develop strong core muscles, you reduce your chance of injury and increase your stability. You enjoy these benefits only after you've worked on your abs and obliques. You need to decide if the pain of doing nothing exceeds the pain of doing something.

To achieve the results you want, you must be willing to work on the supporting processes.

A manufacturer wants to make an innovative, high-quality product at a competitive price. This product comes after the product has been designed, engineered, and tested.

A services firm wants to help and delight its clients. This delight comes after the service has been developed, the value explained, and the new client brought on board.

A non-profit wants to help more constituents. This ability comes after raising funds, balancing the budget, hiring the right people, and training volunteers.

A software company wants to develop raving fans who would never consider canceling their software subscription. This loyalty comes after squashing the software bugs, training the customers, and answering tech support questions.

A private school wants to produce well-prepared graduates who exemplify the school's mission. This happens only after the applications have been received, the tuition paid, the teachers hired and trained, and the classrooms prepared.

You may think, "I'm working on something else that's urgent... it's not a good time. I don't have time to work on this." It's never a convenient time. There's always something else you could be working on: completing projects, responding to customers, helping team members, adopting new technology, or pursuing new ideas. Don't let the pursuit of convenience crowd out the opportunity to make lasting, positive change.

If you're struggling to survive and don't have a minute to spare, the Process Prescription can help. You can start small with the Process Prescription and make progress step-by-step. You don't have to do everything all at once.

Key Ingredient #3: You're willing to develop a process culture

Are you willing to move to the next level of operational excellence, even if things are running "well enough" at your organization? If so, the Process Prescription provides a pathway.

You need to be willing to develop a culture that respects people and encourages process improvement. By culture, I mean a set of core beliefs that result in specific behaviors. Strive for a deep commitment to improvement that is ingrained into everything you do: how you hire, how you train, how you work, and how you pursue innovation.

The Air Safety Institute helps companies develop a healthy culture and good habits related to flight safety. They put it this way, "A safety culture is not a checklist item; it is a way of operating that pays attention to the details."[5]

Paul Akers is an entrepreneur, business owner, and inventor based in Washington state. His company, FastCap, manufactures and distributes unique woodworking products to customers worldwide. In his book *2 Second Lean*, he says, "everything is a process, and everything must be improved."[6]

When Paul was asked, "How do I become lean and run my department better?" he provided clear advice: "First, you must understand one thing. Everything you do in your digital world is a process. Everything I do in my manufacturing world is a process:

- How I set up a machine
- How I clean a machine
- How I clean the toilet
- How I organize my tools
- How I communicate with my team

Everything is a process. I'm performing hundreds, if not thousands, of processes every day."

Paul doesn't stop there. He goes further: "99% of every process you do is clunky."[7] Paul's admonition can spur us to action: as we develop a process culture, we must be willing to train our "process eye" to find ways to improve. Pick the easiest things to improve first. Start with the low-hanging fruit, and be willing to persevere when the fruit becomes harder to reach.

FastCap is a manufacturing company. What if your business is nothing like Paul's? What if you don't make things? Let's say you run a non-profit youth center that provides after-school programs. That's completely different, right?

Here's one example of how these businesses are similar: when something breaks, it affects their ability to serve their customers. If FastCap's injection molding machine breaks, they can't make plastic parts. At the youth center, if the ping-pong table breaks, the students can't have fun playing ping-pong. The equipment needs to work in both of these completely different organizations.

The youth center could develop a guide for "How to maintain the ping-pong table" with the following sections:

- How to fix the net
- How to order new equipment (paddles, balls, net)

- How to fold and store the table

This guide could be expanded to become "How to manage the rec room equipment", which could include more helpful explanations:

- How to get something repaired
- How to buy and replace equipment (retailers, required features, cost)
- How to maintain and clean the equipment

Checklist for understanding the benefits of the Process Prescription

☐ Recognize that the people in your business get work done by running a collection of processes. Improving your processes improves your business.

☐ Identify needs in your organization related to consistency, results, people, and timeliness.

☐ Be willing to develop a process culture by investing the required thought, time, and effort.

Chapter 2

Why the Process Prescription Works

Now that we've identified the ingredients for success, let's look at why the Process Prescription works.

Process-focused or unfocused?

Think of the companies that you respect. What are your favorite stores and restaurants? Behind the scenes, they're process-focused. Many restaurants are run by franchisees. The parent franchisor company licenses a set of processes to the franchisees so they can replicate the founder's success.

A company that wants to scale up must focus on processes in order to repeat early successes and isolate failures. A forward-thinking company must focus on processes to prepare for a variety of "what's next" scenarios.

When organizations are *not* process-focused, problems abound: it's a struggle to ship products on time, customer support is inconsistent, and team members wonder if their contribution makes a difference.

Wisdom from Business Leaders

Let's hear from some leading business minds about why you should embrace process thinking. These leaders speak to the benefits of documenting your processes, creating systems, and setting standards.

Peter Drucker was a leading business strategist of the last century. He wrote 39 books and advised leaders at many organizations, including General Motors, IBM, and the Salvation Army. He wrote this about capturing knowledge:

> "Few questions force a management into as objective, as searching, as productive a look at itself as the question: What is our specific knowledge? Few answers, moreover, are as important as the answer to this question. Knowledge itself is a perishable commodity. It has to be reaffirmed, relearned, repracticed all the time. One has to work constantly at regaining one's specific excellence. But how can one work at maintaining one's excellence unless one knows what it is?"[1]

Michael Gerber authored several books on entrepreneurship and founded a consulting business to help small business owners. He wrote,

> "Once you recognize the purpose of your life is not to serve your business, but that the primary purpose of your business is to serve your life, you can then go to work *on* your business, rather than in it, with a full of why it is absolutely necessary for you to do so."[2]

He also explained that documentation "designates the purpose of the work, specifies the steps needed to be taken while doing that work, and summarizes the standards associated with both the process and the result."[3]

Sam Carpenter, author and business owner, applied process thinking to his telephone answering company. According to Sam,

> "There is some sit-down work as you create documentation in order to better define your targets and to keep moving efficiently toward them. It's a superb investment because the end product will be a relaxed persona, plenty of money, and lots of free time. In all probability, it will be the best investment of time you will ever make. (Boring but true: what is the single major operational difference between a large successful business and a small struggling one? Intense system management.)"[4]

Gino Wickman took over his family's troubled business at age 25. He turned it around and eventually sold the company. Key to his success was his reliance on process. He says, "No matter how many core processes you have, you need to identify the ones that address every activity going on in the business."[5]

These leaders understand the value of working with systems and processes. The Process Prescription begins with these concepts and expands them with details on how to strengthen your business.

Now let's explore some specific reasons why the Process Prescription works.

The Process Prescription reduces risk

We like surprises when we're young: Birthdays! Gifts! Parties! But when we're older, business surprises aren't as exciting. Surprises often reveal unknown risks or bad things we hoped wouldn't happen.

Instead of being tossed back and forth by unfortunate events, we want to build a resilient and durable business that can withstand internal and external surprises. We can't avoid all risks, but we can work to prevent and mitigate losses.

The Process Prescription helps you identify and label your riskiest processes, contributing risk factors, and potential loss. Risks stem from various sources:

- Mistakes by staff or vendors
- Misconduct by employees or contractors
- Macroeconomic factors such as inflation and exchange rates
- Service outages such as power failures
- External forces such as weather
- Organization changes such as mergers
- People changes such as staff departures

After gaining a broad view of risks across your organization, you can develop separate processes to protect your business from catastrophic loss.

Reducing the risk of catastrophic failures

The risk of engine failure is a risk that airlines face every day. But they reduce that risk with processes focused on prevention. With careful observation and the right tools, they can spot warning signs and fix a problem before it takes down an entire jetliner. A turbine blade failure destroys the jet engine and can cut control cables and hydraulic lines as it breaks apart. How do airlines avoid this dangerous problem? They use processes to define how to inspect and test turbine blades. These processes include strict adherence to an inspection schedule. They also monitor how many usage cycles the blades have experienced. They replace high-pressure turbine blades after a specified usage limit before the blades break.

Besides processes for preventing failures, airlines also have processes for recovering from failures. How the flight crew responds to engine failure determines whether the flight ends in a safe landing or a crash.

An airline industry expert put it like this: "Mistakes will happen. They always happen. But our vigilance and the way that we deal with these mistakes is what keeps the industry as safe as it is."[6]

Reducing the risk of human error

The healthcare industry also relies on processes to reduce risk. Hospitals flag the most serious, preventable mistakes to focus special attention on eliminating those errors. In 2001, Dr. Ken Kizer introduced the term "never event." It's something serious but identifiable and preventable, so it should never happen.[7]

An example of a never event is a surgery performed on the wrong body part. Don't laugh; it happens. Another example of a never event is when a surgeon leaves a medical instrument or sponge inside a patient's body after surgery. These tragic and sometimes fatal events are rare, but they do occur. How do doctors and hospitals prevent never events? They take particular precautions when performing risky tasks. They develop and refine processes that disrupt the chain of events that lead to a never event. Their process tools include time-outs, checklists, and verbal verifications.

Reducing the impact of disruptions

Bad things happen, but the Process Prescription can help prepare for disruptions and help you recover faster.

Mitigate disruptions by having a "how to survive this" process. For example, a sudden employee departure could be a major or minor disturbance, depending on your preparation. If the employee's process knowledge is already captured in How-to Guides, then the departure is no big deal. A new person can step in and fill the vacated role. How-to Guides also help with planned absences such as vacations and parental leave. A substitute can take over someone's role temporarily.

If not managed well, a rare event could be serious. For example, a drunk airline passenger starts threatening others on the plane. This situation isn't something the flight crew *wants* to deal with, but they must be prepared for such an event. Flight attendants learn to apply the right process when dealing with disruptive passengers. For these types of events, it's important to know what to do, what to say, and when to get help.

The Process Prescription increases people's happiness

You need to take care of the people affected by your organization. Your team members, clients, and suppliers are vital to your success. Toyota calls this approach "people first."

People are more important than processes, since processes are useless without people to run them. And processes are designed to benefit people, not vice versa.

The solution is to focus on people *and* process. Respect people and rely on them to implement and improve their processes.

In an article titled "7 Reasons to Prioritize Attention to Your Team Ahead of Procedure," Martin Zwilling makes a case for focusing on your team more than on processes.[8]

Here's what Zwilling recommends so that we don't over-focus on processes:

- Share your values and goals effectively

- Select 'A' players
- Provide adequate training
- Help team members stay engaged and focused
- Learn from mistakes
- Implement continual improvement
- Look for innovative ideas
- Analyze customer feedback
- Take risks

Ironically, you can avoid process overload with—you guessed it—a process. Instead of saying, "it's about people, not process," a more refined view would be, "it's about people processes, *then* the other processes." Zwilling's helpful insight is that the sequence of creating and building processes matters.

Put people first. Give people careful attention, but don't ignore your processes.

But how do you put people first? How do you create a work environment that fosters happiness?

Taylor Smith founded Blueboard, a firm that helps companies recognize and incentivize their people. He identified five things that people who love their jobs have in common.[9] Here's his list:

1. They know what's expected of them
2. They make a real impact
3. They feel recognized
4. They enjoy their coworkers
5. They're proud to work where they do

The Process Prescription sets expectations (#1) by clarifying what everyone should be doing. The Process Prescription helps people make a real impact (#2) by providing a means for everyone to contribute by making incremental, frequent improvements. You can create a system for recognizing and encouraging your team members (#3), which you refine year after year. You develop a healthy "people first" culture when everyone's skills are valued, sharpened, and shared. The outcome is better teamwork (#4) and a sense of pride in what the team is creating (#5).

We can also consider how the Process Prescription is an antidote to three thieves of happiness.

- **Stress.** People don't like ambiguity and uncertainty since it leads to stressful situations. Instead, provide clarity. Let people know what they are supposed to do. Create an always-current job description for each role that lists every assigned process for that role.
- **Wasted effort.** People don't like spending time on things that don't matter. Instead, make sure all actions are focused on validated, necessary processes.
- **Frustration.** People don't like having the same annoyances appear again and again. Instead, involve your team members in solving these irritations. Allow them to develop and describe the best methods to avoid frustration.

Use the Process Prescription to flip the script and turn each problem into an opportunity. This way of thinking is not a naïve, wishful approach. Instead,

- Treat every frustration as an opportunity to refine a process.
- Treat every mistake as an opportunity to understand the cause and minimize the chance of recurrence.
- Treat every failure as an opportunity to reject something that doesn't work.
- Treat every question as an opportunity to improve how you communicate.

The Process Prescription reduces tedium and keeps things interesting

Nobody likes to think of themselves as a tiny cog in a giant machine. People are not meant to be robots. But we all have to do things that are tedious or boring. Since we can't escape these repetitive tasks, why not complete them as quickly as possible? Then we can focus on our more enjoyable and valuable tasks.

Identifying and assigning processes does not turn people into mindless robots. It's quite the opposite. By documenting routine work, you free up time and energy, so your team members can focus on the human side of the business: caring for customers and finding new ways to meet their needs.

If you can complete a repetitive, robot-like task faster, then you have more time to improve your business and share your knowledge of how processes work.

After you identify and standardize a repetitive task, give that task to a robot! Free the humans to work on higher-value tasks. Simple software robots can send reminders, parse messages, and process files. On the factory floor, hardware robots can move things and make things. Or devise new machines or programs to help you do repetitive tasks with less effort.

The Process Prescription reduces mental clutter. It frees your mind to work on more challenging projects and more valuable tasks. So instead of "cogs in a machine," we are "vital components in multiple, improving systems."

Though it's not possible to remove all boredom and tedium from work. It is work, after all. But if your people can develop an ability to work *on* their jobs, not just *in* their jobs, then work becomes more interesting.

The Process Prescription makes work visible

The Process Prescription is like an x-ray for your business. One summer, my 12-year-old son was horsing around by replacing the stuffing in a giant teddy bear with himself. I don't recommend this. He started dancing on one foot, lost his balance, and toppled over. Unable to catch himself, he hit the floor hard on his left side and was in immediate pain. He lay on the floor, unwilling to move. We rushed him to the emergency room. We knew something was wrong, but what was the exact problem? Did he need surgery? Could there be complications? He got an x-ray, and the doctor diagnosed a broken collarbone. We learned that the pain would subside, and my son would need to wear a sling for a few weeks. The injury would heal without surgery. What a huge relief!

With the visibility provided by the x-ray, the doctor provided a calm diagnosis and treatment plan.

Now consider an undocumented process in your business that breaks repeatedly or one that does not get completed properly. You feel the process pain, but do you know what's causing it? Are you able to answer the following questions?

- What exactly happens?
- When and where does this problem happen?
- Does it break in the same place every time? What's happening before it breaks? Are there any warning signs that this problem will happen?
- How often does this problem happen?
- Who encounters this problem?
- What are the root causes of this problem?
- Is this problem due to internal causes (something we do) or external causes (something someone else does)?
- What control do we have over the causes?

Manufacturers have a head start answering these questions since they can see a broken machine or a malfunctioning part. But it's more difficult to see what led to a lost sale, an upset customer, a misplaced document, or an incorrect calculation.

Use the Process Prescription to define processes even if you're working with data and not physical things. You can still document each step to visualize the process.

Creating a "How-to Guide" allows everyone who runs a process to follow the same instructions and get consistent results. Anyone can suggest improvements based on customer needs, new ideas, and resolved problems. Refinements get added to the How-to Guide for easy access.

With this added visibility, you have a clear path to repeatability.

The Process Prescription improves results

The Process Prescription allows you to scale up by finding and fixing constraints.

For example, a team at a roofing contractor can describe the best way to replace a roof quickly with a high level of customer satisfaction. Having that process documented results in faster completion and less rework. As they standardize the easy stuff, team members can spend more time solving more rewarding challenges, such as getting more profitable projects or expanding to other locations.

Analyze your processes based on their financial impact. Build on your most effective processes. Streamline, automate, or eliminate your worst processes.

The Process Prescription increases the value of your business

The Process Prescription creates value by capturing your valuable know-how. You can sell this intellectual property or pass it down to the next generation.

Michael Gerber describes developing systems and processes as building the "franchise prototype." To franchise or sell your business, you need to capture how things are done. Your equipment, software, and facilities don't run themselves. You create value for your customers when the right people are running the right processes. You need to capture the "Brainware" that makes everything work together.

If your business relies on information workers, then what's in their brains is a large part of your company's value. This valuable information includes plans, ideas, to-do lists, techniques, and productivity hacks. As Bill Gates described it, "The inventory, the value of my company, walks out the door every evening."

It will be painful losing a genius programmer or a superstar sales executive. But you can reduce this pain using the Process Prescription. You can capture how those high performers achieve superior results in How-to Guides. If you need to hire a replacement, find someone who is smart, coachable, and ready to tackle bigger challenges. Your new hire will benefit from having documentation about how things work and how to get results. They can improve the How-to Guide by adding details, recurring scenarios, and answers to common questions. Repeat this routine with all your new hires, and your processes will get better and better. You'll be creating valuable intellectual property that increases the value of your business.

The Process Prescription shares knowledge

The Process Prescription encourages collaboration. When you create an easy-to-access repository for all your processes, your team can contribute their knowledge about each process.

Create easy-to-share How-to Guides that capture the best way to run each process. Does something not work? Is it confusing or prone to error? Make a note and edit the process. That way, your processes keep getting smoother. Productivity improves gradually and methodically.

Computer programmers use the abbreviation DRY, which stands for Don't Repeat Yourself. Smart programmers reuse computer code by creating functions and modules that they reference in new programs. This approach isn't laziness; it's efficiency.

I asked one of my consulting clients how he creates a project proposal for a new customer. He explained, "My process for creating a proposal? It's easy. I reuse one of our old proposals and email it to them." This method is a step in the right direction since he was reusing, and not re-creating, an existing document. But as we talked more, we found parts of his process that he reinvented each time, such as how to change the proposal to meet different client needs. He was also making undocumented choices about how to contact the client, how to follow up with the client, how to return the signed agreement, and how to kick off a new customer project.

He was using a few templates, plus a lot of his memory. A better method would be to capture and reuse all of his expert knowledge by creating a guide called "How to create and send a project proposal." The document would capture all the variations and suggestions for creating an effective proposal.

A note on terminology: I prefer the term "How-to Guide" to describe documentation for a process, but there are several other names for these documents, such as Standard Operating Procedures, Action Plans, Job

Aids, Work Instructions, Knowledge Articles, Frameworks, and Methodologies.

What should you call your entire collection of How-to Guides? I prefer the name "Process Library." But you can call this repository your Playbook, Runbook, Operations Manual, Policy Manual, Knowledgebase, Catalog, Repository, Resource Library, or Wiki.

So I'll refer to "a Process Library that contains How-to Guides."

The Process Prescription accelerates training

The Process Prescription defines the roles in your organization. Then you assign processes to each role. New team members can see everything they need to do in a new role. For example, the new Accounts Receivable Manager knows the exact list of 12 processes that are her responsibility. She can ask questions and make clarifying notes as she learns these processes. She gets up to speed faster and has fewer surprises.

Use your list of processes to build competency-based training. Each process can link to relevant training resources, such as videos, articles, and online courses. You can create your own learning modules to teach how processes should be run. These learning modules can include how to get started and how to handle more advanced scenarios.

Once trained, new employees should know how to run each of their processes. They can go back and redo the relevant training modules if they need some review. Encourage them to improve the training by capturing unanswered questions and making suggestions

You can cross-train team members, so two people can swap roles for a specified period. Each person gets a wider variety of roles and a more interesting mix of work. You're also developing a backup person for each role. This multi-skilling or job rotation allows different people to learn and run the same process, so you iron out problems and inconsistencies faster.

The Process Prescription standardizes work

Applying the Process Prescription creates a standard way of doing things, so things get done faster. You can use this extra time to find improvements, reduce stress, or increase output.

If something goes wrong, find the root causes and implement a fix that benefits everyone using that process in the future.

Consider your interaction with businesses that do not have consistent, standard processes. For example, let's say I go to a certain restaurant that is usually fabulous, but on 20% of my visits, I receive poor service. I won't take someone there for a business lunch, since I'm not sure it will be a good experience. Why risk it? Consistency is key.

The Process Prescription provides accountability

The Process Prescription clarifies the ownership of every process and task. You remove the ambiguity about who should be doing what, when, and how. You create a chain of clarity:

- Each person has one or more roles.
- Each role owns a collection of processes.
- Each process generates tasks and due dates.

A person works on tasks based on processes they own. The Process Prescription helps everyone remember when things are due and how to do them. With this type of accountability, no recurring task should slip through the cracks.

The Process Prescription spurs continuous improvement

The Japanese word *kaizen* embodies the idea of continuous improvement. The word *kaizen* comes from the words *kai* (meaning 'change') and *zen* (meaning 'good'). In other words, what can we change for the better?

The Process Prescription allows you to speed up the flow of improvement ideas from your team members' brains into their daily workflows.

You can find and improve processes that should be faster. You can identify wasted effort. You can automate the boring stuff. You can apply technology and tools to make things easier.

Checklist for understanding why the Process Prescription works

- [ ] List the types of disruptions that your business could experience.
- [ ] Consider how written processes could improve your readiness to face these challenges.
- [ ] List frustrations that people face when dealing with your business. These people could be employees, contractors, customers, suppliers, or partners.
- [ ] Consider how written processes could simplify interactions and reduce frustration.
- [ ] List the types of information that your business consumes and generates.
- [ ] Consider how written processes could provide more value to customers by streamlining and organizing your information.

Chapter 3

How to Use This Book

We've investigated the reasons behind the Process Prescription and the benefits of the Process Prescription. Now that we've explored the Why, let's dig into the How.

The overall objective of the Process Prescription is simple: to optimize your processes and strengthen your business.

The main steps of the Process Prescription boil down to four verbs: Identify, Describe, Use, and Improve.

Each step represents a leap forward in process discovery and improvement. In the coming chapters, we'll cover how to implement the Process Prescription for your business using these Four Steps.

Figure 3-1. Upcoming Chapters. Use each chapter to apply part of the step-by-step Process Prescription.

Identify	Describe	Use	Improve
Chapter 4. Identify Your **Functional Areas**		Chapter 10. Use Your Processes in **Day-to-Day Work**	Chapter 13. **Improve** Your Processes
Chapter 5. Identify Your **Roles**	Chapter 8. Describe Your Processes With **Attributes**	Chapter 11. Use Your Processes With **Your Team**	Chapter 14. Improve Your Processes by **Learning from Others**
Chapter 6. Identify Your **Processes**	Chapter 9. Describe Your Processes Using **How-To Guides**	Chapter 12. Use Your Processes With **Business Frameworks**	Chapter 15. Improve Your Processes Using **External Resources**
Chapter 7. Identify **Gaps and Opportunities**			

Step 1 - Identify your Processes

The first step focuses on understanding what your organization does. We'll create an inventory of the processes that your organization uses to get work done. It's important to get full visibility of everything before you start improving things. This process inventory reveals priorities, relationships, overlaps, duplications, and gaps.

We find what needs to change to make your business healthier. A doctor collects a patient's vital signs, family history, and blood test results. Careful assessment allows for an accurate diagnosis and treatment plan. Likewise, your business benefits from having a fuller picture of what's going on. A systematic review of your processes allows you to see what's happening across your entire organization.

The Process Prescription is a pathway to discover your processes and uncover the knowledge that exists throughout your organization. We'll look at the main areas of your business and the roles and activities within each area.

After completing Step 1, you will have done the following:

- Identified all your processes

- Created a role-based organizational chart
- Created a Process Library. This inventory allows you to create a list of processes for each role and prioritize what needs improvement.

Processes vs. Tasks

For clarity, we need to distinguish a process from a task. If a process is a recipe for getting work done, what's a "task?" In this book, we'll consider a task to be the act of following a process one time through.

Think of the process as the cookie recipe that can be used multiple times. A task is when you use that recipe to bake a batch of cookies. The process is the template you follow when completing a task. You can follow a written process as often as you need.

A recurring parent process, such as "how to send invoices," will generate multiple child tasks over time. If you invoice monthly, that one process will create a new task each month.

Figure 3-2. Parent Processes. Create child tasks based on parent process.

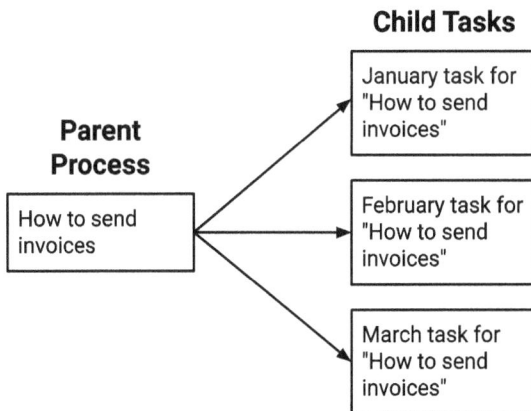

Processes vs. Projects

Let's also distinguish a process from a project. If a process is a recipe for getting work done, how's that different from a project?

A project is a large task, a complex task, or a collection of tasks. Projects tend to have multiple work streams and require coordination between multiple people. Projects usually have a one-time focus rather being part of routine operations. For example, "migrating to a new accounting system" is a project, while "running the monthly bookkeeping" is a routine task.

Most projects are similar to something that's been done before. For this reason, projects should still be run according to a process. Even a "special" or unusual project should follow a process in one of these ways:

- Apply proven project management methods to complete the project.
- Hire a specialist who has already perfected the process that you need.
- Create a more generic version of the project and define that process. Using the example from above, if "migrating to a new accounting system" is something you plan to do once and then never again, you should still create and follow a process for "how to migrate to a new software system" since that has a decent chance of happening again.
- Recognize that your special project belongs to a group of similar projects that do indeed reoccur. Create a process for this broader category of projects, and include instructions for completing projects based on different scenarios.

Here's the hierarchy that we'll use in this book:

- **Process**, which is the overall method to achieve a result or complete a routine.
  - **Task**, which is the defined work needed to run a process one-time through. A larger task could also be called a project.
    - **Step**, which is a specific action needed to complete part of a task. This could also be called a subtask.

An entire genre of software has emerged to manage projects by tracking assignments and deadlines. But these project tools should work with process tools that describe and refine the underlying processes that allow you to complete the projects.

Step 2 - Describe your Processes

The second step adds more detail about your processes and how they work.

Adding descriptors and labels to each process allows you to prioritize processes based on value and risk. You can also evaluate your progress by adding labels for processes that are fully documented, partly documented, or not documented at all.

As you describe your processes in more detail, you capture the best ways to deal with common problems. You spend less time fighting fires and dealing with recurring annoyances.

In this step, you add How-to Guides with step-by-step instructions for running your processes and completing tasks. You don't have to document every process in excruciating detail, but you should capture the basic steps to complete each process.

Step 3 - Use your Processes

At this step, your team follows How-to Guides for their assigned processes to complete their day-to-day work.

Your How-to Guides include steps to follow and checklists for verifying your work. As you run your processes, make notes of problems and look for ways to improve. Have different people use the same process to make sure the process is understandable. Refine your How-to Guides by resolving ambiguities and inaccuracies.

Completing Step 3 helps scale up your operations since you've captured know-how in a set of replicable instructions. You can now add customers and new team members in a steady, predictable way.

Step 4 - Improve your Processes

At this step, you explore ways to improve your processes. Make your processes faster, less expensive, more consistent, easier, more enjoyable, less risky, and less error-prone.

When working on Step 4, you're using your documented processes and finding ways to optimize them.

Checklist for using the four steps in this book

- ☐ Start where you are to organize and optimize your processes. Apply the four steps in sequence since they build on each other to maximize results.

- ☐ Complete Step 1 (Identify) to prevent working on just your favorite processes, which may not be the most important. Chapters 4 through 7 cover this.

- ☐ Complete Step 2 (Describe) to create reusable guides and capture the knowledge needed to complete work. Chapters 8 and 9 cover this.

- ☐ Complete Step 3 (Use) to make sure your documentation does not become stale and irrelevant. Chapters 10 through 12 cover this.

- ☐ Complete Step 4 (Improve) to benefit from your hard work in the previous steps. Find new ways to improve results, reduce risk, and grow faster. Chapters 13 through 15 cover this.

Chapter 4

How to Identify Your Functional Areas

Identify	Describe	Use	Improve
Chapter 4. Identify Your **Functional Areas**		Chapter 10. Use Your Processes in **Day-to-Day Work**	Chapter 13. **Improve** Your Processes
Chapter 5. Identify Your **Roles**	Chapter 8. Describe Your Processes With **Attributes**	Chapter 11. Use Your Processes With **Your Team**	Chapter 14. Improve Your Processes by **Learning from Others**
Chapter 6. Identify Your **Processes**	Chapter 9. Describe Your Processes Using **How-To Guides**	Chapter 12. Use Your Processes With **Business Frameworks**	Chapter 15. Improve Your Processes Using **External Resources**
Chapter 7. Identify **Gaps and Opportunities**			

The first step in applying the Process Prescription is to identify the functional areas of your business. This chapter aims to identify five to nine functional areas that fully encapsulate everything your business or department does. This is similar to naming your various groups or sections, but we are aiming for a special list of categories covering every aspect of your business without overlap. This will help when we identify your processes.

What is a functional area?

A functional area is a high-level category of activities in your organization.

For example, a private school might have these six functional areas:
- Finance
- Facilities
- Programs
- Advancement
- Governance
- Staffing

A software company might have these seven:
- Finance
- Information Technology
- Research & Development
- Sales & Marketing
- Human Resources
- Operations
- Project Management

Your business's functional areas will depend on what you make and sell and how you run your business.

What are the benefits of using functional areas?

A list of your functional areas is the foundation for identifying and organizing your processes. Using functional areas allows you to do the following:
- Focus your attention using these logical groups of activity. Look at all the items in each area to find common themes and new ways to improve. This is similar to the way a home inspector organizes an inspection of a home's systems: electrical, plumbing, exterior, roofing, foundation, and HVAC.

- Get a complete overview of your business with a list of just five to nine areas. Use this short list of areas to explain your business prospects, customers, employees, new hires, lenders, vendors, or anyone who needs a quick overview. You can also use your list of functional areas to organize budgeting, planning, reviews, and board meetings.
- Align these functional areas with your current organizational chart. By seeing everything your business does in a single view, you may find ways to simplify by combining or reassigning functions.
- Organize your process documentation by functional area. Each process belongs to one functional area. Your Process Library becomes a valuable resource with quick access to any topic.

Creating a list of functional areas for your business is similar to how libraries use categories to organize the world's knowledge. The Dewey Decimal System, used by over 200,000 libraries, has ten categories ranging from the 000s (computer science, information, and general works) to the 900s (history and geography).

Don't worry about functional areas becoming independent silos. Your teams can work and collaborate across multiple functional areas as needed. You can define roles that are responsible for a collection of processes in different functional areas. You can also define pathways or value chains that link multiple processes to achieve a bigger goal.

You get a bird's-eye view of your organization when you identify your functional areas. This high-level view can help you generate ideas for sharing resources, finding opportunities, and developing a culture of process thinking.

How to brainstorm a draft list of your functional areas

To start identifying your functional areas, create a list of all the departments, sections, and types of activities in your business. Start with a rough list. Just write down whatever you can think of. It's okay if you have too many areas to start. You can refine your list as you work through this step.

Let's look at five possible resources for creating a rough list of your functional areas: your organizational chart, the Make-Market-Manage framework, a list of C-suite titles, a generic template, and ready-to-go lists.

Use whichever of these brainstorming methods works best to create a draft list of all your organization's functional areas. Or try them all. Don't worry about having too many functional areas on your list. We'll refine your list after this brainstorming step.

Use your Organizational Chart or Staff Roster

Your organizational chart ("org chart") is a good first place to look since that identifies your team members and their areas of responsibility. The way you group people to work together can give you a draft list of your functional areas. Add groups and departments from your org chart to your list of functional areas.

If you don't have an org chart, make a list of all the people who work for your organization. This list should include employees, contractors, and consultants. Each group or category on this list could represent a functional area.

Use Make-Market-Manage

One way to think of your business functions at a high level is Make-Market-Manage. The general idea is that most organizations need to do three basic things:

1. **Make:** create a product or service for your customers (or clients, members, students).
2. **Market:** sell your products and services and get new customers. This includes converting inquiries into new paying customers, selling more to existing customers, and acquiring new customers. A non-profit organization could call this "Fund it" if they rely on donors and don't charge directly for their services.
3. **Manage:** running your business' finances and infrastructure. This involves tracking the money and people, as well as other things needed to operate your business.

But having these three functional areas is too broad—there are too many different things to do in each area. Instead, split each of these three areas into two or three more areas. Aim for five to nine total functional areas, with six or seven being ideal.

Here's a list of possible functional areas based on the Make-Market-Manage categories.

Make: fulfill customer requests, meet client needs

1. Research: convert raw ideas into new product ideas
2. Design & Development: create new products and improve old ones
3. Testing: validate your product's readiness
4. Production and Service Delivery: make the product and serve your customers
5. Customer Support: assist your customers and answer their questions
6. Logistics: store, schedule, and deliver products to customers

Market: get new orders and new customers

7. Channel and Partner Development: find other organizations to help you sell
8. Marketing and Lead Generation: generate new inquiries
9. Branding: develop and improve awareness of your organization in the marketplace
10. Sales: help customers buy your product or service
11. Development and Fundraising: find benefactors or investors for your business

Manage: run the business

12. Human Resources: hire, onboard, train, and offboard people
13. Finance: spend money, collect payments, track money, invest money
14. Facilities: manage the space and equipment that your team needs
15. Legal: meet legal requirements, create agreements
16. Information Technology: build and maintain the technology infrastructure

17. Leadership: set strategy and objectives; help navigate around obstacles
18. Governance: update owners or board members; receive guidance
19. Compliance and Risk Management: recognize and mitigate risks
20. Administration: group multiple "Manage" functions into this area
21. Infrastructure: group multiple "Manage" functions into this area

Pick just the areas that are relevant to your business. If nearly all of these apply to you, that's fine. In the next section, we'll see how to simplify this list by combining some of your smaller areas. The goal is to get your list of functional areas down to a manageable list of five to nine items.

Use C-Suite job titles

In large companies, the C-Suite or executive team defines the functional areas of the business since each area needs a Chief to manage it. For example, common C-Suite (or "CxO") titles include the following:

- Chief Executive Officer
- Chief Financial Officer
- Chief Operating Officer
- Chief Information Officer
- Chief Technology Officer

But even in a smaller organization, thinking about C-Suite job titles may provide ideas for naming your functional areas. Here are some additional types of Chief Officers:

- Revenue (Business Development, Growth, Sales)
- Human Resources Officer (People)
- Information Security (Privacy)
- Compliance (Risk)
- Knowledge
- Customer
- Strategy
- Investment
- Marketing (Brand)
- Product

- Procurement (Sourcing, Supply Chain)
- Logistics
- Quality
- Administrative (Accounting)

Use a generic template

There are some areas that are common to nearly all businesses. Finance is one example. If your organization deals with money, then you have a Finance functional area. The acronym FA-SHRIMP describes a list of eight common functional areas:

- Finance. Most companies treat this as a separate functional area.
- Administration. This can include processes not covered by other areas in this list, such as office reception.
- Sales. In a smaller organization, you can combine this area with marketing.
- Human Resources. This includes hiring, training, and managing benefits.
- Research & Development. This includes the processes for preparing a product or service for production.
- Infrastructure. This can include information technology and facilities.
- Marketing. In a smaller organization, you can combine this area with sales.
- Production. This can include manufacturing or providing services to customers. A school could call this area Programs or Academics. An accounting firm could call this Client Services.

Use ready-to-go lists

You can use a list of functional areas from a business that is similar to yours. Start with a ready-to-go list that's specific to your type of business, then modify it to meet your needs.

Below are some examples of functional areas for different types of organizations.

A private school might have six functional areas: Finance, Facilities, Programs, Advancement (marketing, admissions, fundraising), Governance, and Staffing. Recall these areas using the mnemonic FF-PAGS.

A real estate firm could use FAM-SHS: Finance, Administration and Infrastructure, Marketing, Sales, Human Resources, and Service.

A non-profit could use DCF-GAP: Development, Communications, Finance, Governance, Administration, and Programs.

A cleaning company could use H-FOAM: Human Resources, Finance, Operations, Admin, Marketing & Sales.

A home accessories store could use MDS-FMFM: (unfortunately, not all the lists form a memorable acronym!): Merchandising, Design, Staffing, Finance, Marketing & Sales, Facilities, and Management.

As you develop your list of functional areas, every activity within your organization should fall into one of your functional areas. Individual product or service lines might need to be considered as separate functional areas based on how your business is run. More ready-to-go lists are available at ProcessPrescription.com.

How to create functional areas for a department

If you're responsible for one department in a larger organization, you can create functional areas for just your department. For example, a marketing department could be run using CASED:

- Content Marketing & Lead Generation
- Advertising
- Search Optimization & Analytics
- Events & Projects
- Direct Marketing

A legal department at a large company could be run using ICE COLA functional areas:

- Intellectual Property
- Contracts
- External Affairs
- Compliance

- Operations
- Litigation
- Administration

These areas would be under the leadership of the legal department's senior executive, the General Counsel. Some of the work within each functional area might be outsourced to a law firm, but each area would still require in-house oversight.

How to refine your list of functional areas

Now that you have a draft list of functional areas, let's refine it to create your final list.

Try to keep the number of functional areas at "7 plus or minus 2"

Using just three areas (make it, market it, manage it) to describe your business is too simplistic. But then, if using dozens of areas is too complex, what's the right number of areas?

Psychology research has shown that our short-term memory is limited to about seven items, plus or minus two.[1]

"Seven, plus or minus two" gives us a range of five to nine functional areas. This seems about right since we want an easy way to remember all the areas of our business. Five to nine may also be a reasonable number of direct reports for your top executive.

Use subareas

"But wait," you say, "I can't just clump all my money-related processes under one giant 'Finance' area. We do lots of financial things!"

If you find yourself needing more detail, use subareas to describe what happens within a particular functional area. For example, your Finance area could include the subareas of Accounts Payable, Accounts Receivable, Payroll, Cash Management & Investments, Taxes, and Bookkeeping.

A "Sales & Marketing" functional area could include the subareas of Advertising, Partnerships & Promotions, Events, Content Marketing, and Outbound Marketing.

Subareas can also be used to capture variations based on different locations or facilities. For example, Manufacturing could be a functional area, and Assembly Line A and Assembly Line B could be subareas. Sales could be a functional area, with the subareas East Region and Midwest Region. For a school with multiple campuses, "Academics and Programs" could be a functional area, and Campus A and Campus B could be subareas.

As you brainstorm and identify your functional areas, keep a list of all the subareas you identify. These notes will come in handy when we identify individual processes.

Avoid "Other"

Some classification systems use an "Other" for anything that doesn't fit neatly into one of the primary categories. But using "Other" as a functional area is too general and ambiguous. Define a set of meaningful functional areas that cover all of your business activities without using "Other."

Combine functions as needed

Combine similar areas until you have five to nine areas of similar importance and breadth. For example, a family-owned law firm with long-time employees won't have many HR processes since they don't hire or fire much. Their Human Resources functions could be contained within their "Admin" area. But a staffing firm that focuses exclusively on HR-related processes might need three functional areas for HR (Recruiting, Training, and Placement) since those are distinct functions of their business.

In a smaller organization with fewer people and moving parts, combine similar areas to create a simpler set of functional areas. For example,

- Marketing and Sales combine well since they contain complementary activities.

- Infrastructure could combine the Manage functions of facilities, maintenance, and information technology. All of these share the theme of providing a firm foundation for your people to be productive.
- Administration can combine the Manage functions of human resources, legal, information technology, and other functions not directly related to Make or Market.
- For a school, Advancement can combine multiple Market functions: Marketing, Communications, Admissions, and Fundraising. All of these have a common theme of explaining the school's mission and welcoming new people into the school community as students or donors.

Choose area names that work for you

Change the area names based on what fits your organization. The functional areas under the broad Make category can vary based on your industry. The names of these areas will differ for a product or service business. A factory might simply use Manufacturing. A school might call their Make process Academics or Programs. A consulting firm could use Client Advisory or Client Services.

Don't shoehorn a name where it doesn't fit. Early in my career, I heard about a large consulting firm insisting that an oil refinery refers to its core operations as "production" since they were "producing" refined products. But in the oil and gas industry, the word "production" relates to the upstream extraction of hydrocarbons, not downstream refining. Using the word "production" to describe a downstream refinery's core operations would be confusing.

Avoid overlap

Your list of functional areas should be MECE (pronounced "mee see"). MECE stands for "Mutually Exclusive, Collectively Exhaustive." This term was coined by Barbara Minto at McKinsey & Company in the late 1960s.

It's a simple but powerful concept. To be MECE, your list of functional areas must be:

1. Mutually exclusive. Avoid overlap between functional areas by assigning each activity and process to a single functional area. This approach will help when we identify and categorize processes within each functional area.

2. Collectively exhaustive. Don't leave anything out. Your list of functional areas should cover every aspect of your business.

Don't say, "My list of functional areas covers everything we do *except...*" Don't make exceptions. Force yourself to refine your list until your functional areas cover everything without overlap.

Standardize where possible

What if one part of your business (such as a unit, group, location, or facility) is completely different from the other parts of your business?

Isolate the activities that are unique to that area, and try to place the unique aspects in their own subarea within an existing functional area. But if the unique activities can't fit into an existing subarea, then create a new functional area that is specific to that aspect of your business.

As a last resort, you can create a separate set of functional areas for your unique business unit. This effectively treats the business unit as a separate entity with a separate Process Library and separate processes. But that approach may be simpler than trying to merge two different businesses into one Process Library.

An example of finding functional areas

Let's look at a final example of Biblical proportions. In the Old Testament, we see the activities of King David's household in ancient Israel. This passage from 1 Chronicles lists people doing a lot of different things:

"And Azmaveth the son of Adiel was over the king's treasuries; and Jehonathan the son of Uzziah was over the storehouses in the field, in the cities, in the villages, and in the fortresses. Ezri the son of Chelub was over those who did the work of the field for tilling the ground.

And Shimei the Ramathite was over the vineyards, and Zabdi the Shiphmite was over the produce of the vineyards for the supply of wine. Baal-Hanan the Gederite was over the olive trees and the sycamore trees that were in the lowlands, and Joash was over the store of oil. And Shitrai the Sharonite was over the herds that fed in Sharon, and Shaphat the son of Adlai was over the herds that were in the valleys. Obil the Ishmaelite was over the camels, Jehdeiah the Meronothite was over the donkeys, and Jaziz the Hagrite was over the flocks. All these were the officials over King David's property. Also Jehonathan, David's uncle, was a counselor, a wise man, and a scribe; and Jehiel the son of Hachmoni was with the king's sons. Ahithophel was the king's counselor, and Hushai the Archite was the king's companion. After Ahithophel was Jehoiada the son of Benaiah, then Abiathar. And the general of the king's army was Joab."[2]

The passage mentions 19 people doing a variety of jobs. How could the king have organized his leadership team into functional areas?

If we extract the activities from the passage and replace the phrase "was over" with "manage," we can see some categories emerge. We can organize these many activities into six functional areas.

Finance and Logistics: track the money and finished goods
- Manage the treasuries
- Manage the storehouses
- Manage the store of oil

Agricultural Services: grow and harvest produce
- Manage the workers of the field who tilled the ground
- Manage the vineyards
- Manage the olive trees and sycamore trees

Manufacturing: create products.
- Produce wine
- Produce olive oil

Management and Training: advise the king and his family
- Create documents as a scribe
- Teach the king's sons

- Counsel the king
- Provide companionship to the king

Animal Care: tend and shepherd the herds of livestock
- Manage the herds that fed in Sharon
- Manage the herds that were in the valleys
- Manage the camels
- Manage the donkeys
- Manage the flocks

Military: protect the country and fight enemies
- Lead the king's army

Checklist for functional areas

To conclude this chapter, here's a summary of how to identify the functional areas in your business.

- ☐ Identify five to nine areas that describe what your business does. Merge or combine areas if needed.
- ☐ Capture the subareas under each functional area
- ☐ Make sure your list of functional areas is MECE.
  - Mutually exclusive: Each activity belongs to only one functional area.
  - Collectively exhaustive: The list of functional areas captures everything we do.

Chapter 5

How to Identify Your Roles

Identify	Describe	Use	Improve
Chapter 4. Identify Your **Functional Areas**	Chapter 8. Describe Your Processes With **Attributes**	Chapter 10. Use Your Processes in **Day-to-Day Work**	Chapter 13. **Improve** Your Processes
Chapter 5. Identify Your **Roles**		Chapter 11. Use Your Processes With **Your Team**	Chapter 14. Improve Your Processes by **Learning from Others**
Chapter 6. Identify Your **Processes**	Chapter 9. Describe Your Processes Using **How-To Guides**		
Chapter 7. Identify **Gaps and Opportunities**		Chapter 12. Use Your Processes With **Business Frameworks**	Chapter 15. Improve Your Processes Using **External Resources**

Now that we've identified functional areas, the next step is to identify the roles that people fill within each area. Having a complete list of functional areas and roles will help us when we identify processes in the next chapter.

What is a role?

A role is a defined function that a person performs. A role is "a part you play" or "a hat you wear." One person can have multiple roles, each with separate responsibilities. For example, one person could simultaneously hold the roles of Office Manager, Payroll Assistant, and Benefits Coordinator.

What roles are needed to implement the Process Prescription?

Before we begin to identify the roles across your entire organization, let's look at three new roles that you'll need to implement the Process Prescription: Process Leader, Process Architect, and Process Pilot.

The Leader casts the vision while supporting and encouraging the other roles. The Architect makes the plan for applying the Process Prescription, and the Pilot implements the plan.

These three roles work together to maximize the benefit of the Process Prescription. The same person can take on more than one of these roles if they have the time and skills.

The Process Leader

The **Leader** is the person in your organization with an entrepreneurial mindset who's willing to build a culture of process thinking. The Process Leader helps your organization apply the Process Prescription by providing the vision, goals, resources, and accountability.

This role could also be called the project sponsor, process champion, lead executive, or visionary.

The Leader role should be filled by someone who understands the benefits of the Process Prescription. They should also be able to prioritize time for themselves and for others to work on the Process Prescription.

The Process Leader may need to allocate only 5% of their time to start, but this effort needs to be a strategic objective with the full commitment of leadership, not just a quick, faddish project. It's important to have support from the top of your organization as you apply the Process Prescription.

As the Process Prescription gains momentum, the Leader can free up more time to focus on strategic process improvements.

Here are some processes that the Process Leader can develop, refine, and implement:

- How to communicate the vision and overall objectives
- How to develop a culture of process improvement
- How to identify and celebrate process successes
- How to resolve roadblocks or obstacles when implementing the Process Prescription
- How to track overall progress across the organization

The Process Architect

The **Architect** defines how the Process Prescription gets implemented within your organization. This role should be filled by someone who can organize the information and people required to implement the Process Prescription.

The Architect role could be filled by an operations person known for getting things done, such as a VP of Operations. If they are too busy, maybe someone on their team could help. Look for someone with the right combination of skills and motivation.

While you could bring in outside help with the Architect role, you can't just hand this book to a consultant and say, "do this!" You must be willing to partner with them and commit the time and resources required.

Here are some processes that the Architect could create:

- How to set up your Process Library hierarchy
- How to set up a naming and labeling system for processes
- How to create and track the implementation timeline
- How to create objectives related to the Process Prescription
- How to create the How-to Guide template
- How to choose and use outside consultants
- How to configure the software for documentation and process improvement
- How to evaluate the results from the Process Prescription

The Process Pilot

The **Pilot** leads the day-to-day process work and navigates your process journey. They make sure things get done and help "land the plane." This person ensures everyone accomplishes their tasks to implement the Process Prescription. This role could also be called Process Builder or Process Coordinator.

The Pilot could also be a small team working together to guide your organization in applying the Process Prescription.

Your Process Pilot could be one of the following:

- Someone who loves structure and organization and is willing to apply the Process Prescription to pull everything together
- A new hire who is eager to learn all the facets of their position
- A long-term employee who has a lot of valuable knowledge and expertise that hasn't been written down
- Your Operations Manager, who is already working on problems that the Process Prescription solves
- Your IT Manager, who already has set up shared folders and resources and wants to help people collaborate better
- A team member who is eager to improve by documenting their processes
- A team in a particular functional area that has a lot of recurring processes, such as Marketing or Finance
- A business owner who wants to start with their own responsibilities and tasks

The Pilot begins with one area or role in your organization and implements the Process Prescription from beginning to end. They work with the Architect to decide how to roll out the Process Prescription more widely within your organization.

Identify a leader in each part of your organization who can partner with the Pilot to implement the Process Prescription.

If you're using a Pilot Team, each team member needs to fully understand the Process Prescription and work through Step 1 (Identify), Step 2 (Describe), and Step 3 (Use) for their own roles. The Pilot Team members can check in with each other weekly to compare notes, share successes, and solve problems. They can continue collaborating and working together on Step 4 (Improve).

The Pilot should find success in one area and then train another Pilot to replicate that success. As long as they are making consistent progress, move at a speed that fits your team best.

Here are some processes for the Pilot to create, document, and complete:

- How to conduct a process identification interview
- How to find top priorities using the Process Library
- How to resolve missing process attributes
- How to create a new How-to Guide for a process that is not documented
- How to train the next group of Process Pilots
- How to enlist new team members to help as needed
- How to set process goals for individuals and groups. This can include how and when to move from Step 1 (identify) to Step 4 (improve).
- How to manage How-to Guides

What are the benefits of using roles?

Begin to define roles separately from the people filling those roles. One person can have multiple, distinct roles. This approach allows you to simplify organizational growth, increase job clarity, and enhance professional development.

Simplify Organizational Growth

Using roles allows you to simplify and accelerate your growth using the "divide and conquer" strategy. A smaller organization may have a Marketing Manager who handles everything related to marketing. But what happens when that person gets too busy and you need to grow your marketing department? You could hire a "Marketing Assistant" to shadow the Marketing Manager, but then what should the assistant do? How does the Marketing Manager carve out some responsibilities for the assistant to handle?

If you think of your marketing function as a collection of roles, you can divide the Marketing Manager role into finer slices that can be assigned to different people. For example, a startup company might have one person filling all of these marketing roles:

- Events Coordinator
- Social Media Coordinator
- Website Coordinator
- Blog Writer
- Video Producer
- Outbound Marketing Coordinator
- Customer Database Administrator

As the startup grows, new part-time or full-time people can take over some of the specific marketing roles. When you reassign a role to a new person, they inherit the set of defined processes for that role. This frees up time for the Marketing Manager to work on other projects.

You can replicate a role if you need more help in an area. For example, if you need another Social Media Coordinator for your growing business, you can reuse that role description when recruiting and hiring.

Increase Job Clarity

Using roles allows you to give each team member 100% clarity on what they should do. Instead of defining someone's job as a list of generic tasks, the Process Prescription clarifies the role and process behind every task by organizing each person's assignments into a logical hierarchy.

Figure 5-1. People to Tasks. Define roles and processes to get more insights and flexibility instead of just assigning tasks to people.

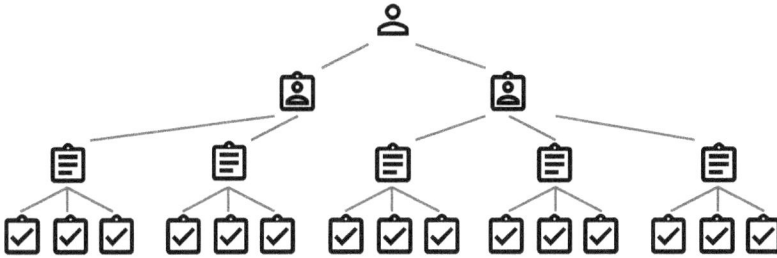

From ♟ **Person to** 🪪 **Role to** 🗐 **Process to** ☑ **Task**

With the Process Prescription, everyone's job is based on their assigned roles, and the specific processes assigned to those roles.

Accelerate Recruiting and Onboarding

Using roles also allows you to refine your recruiting and accelerate your onboarding. You describe a role within a functional area by assigning processes to that role. The list of processes reveals what capabilities someone needs to succeed in that role. It's unclear from just the role name "Assistant Marketing Manager" what the person in that job will be expected to do. But if this role has a list of specific processes, you know what skills will be needed. Once you've clarified all the processes within that role, you may choose to rename the role to something more descriptive such as Social Media Manager.

Enhance Professional Development

Using roles allows you to place people where they can flourish. By defining your organization's roles in detail, you aid people in identifying the roles where they can contribute the most. You can divide broad areas like marketing, sales, and finance into specific roles that appeal to a wider range of personalities, temperaments, and skills. For example, marketing encompasses both creative and analytical roles. If you keep your roles too big and too broad, you may lose the opportunity for people to find areas where they can thrive.

How to identify your organization's roles

Consider each person

For each person in your organization, list all the roles that they fill. List all the distinct hats they wear during a year or during a full cycle of your business operations.

A person's existing job title is a starting point, but this may not fully explain everything they do since people can have multiple roles. The Admissions Director at a small school might also fill the roles of Registrar, Marketing Coordinator, Videographer, Blog Writer, and Administrative Director. This person keeps busy!

The Executive Director at a small non-profit fills many roles. These roles could include Contracts Manager, HR Manager, Office Volunteer Coordinator, Development Committee Chair, and Program Coordinator.

Ask each member of your team, "What are the different types of work that you do? What hats do you wear? What roles do you play?" Write down all their responses to create a list of roles based on what they do. If they have only one role, that's fine. Specialists may focus on one role, while generalists may have several roles.

Consider your functional areas

As a rule of thumb, you should have at least one role that is in charge of each functional area. Depending on the size of your organization, this role could be called a Coordinator, Manager, Director, Vice President, or CxO.

After you name the leadership role for a functional area, identify other roles in that functional area.

For example, the Finance area for a startup could include a Finance Director, Payroll Coordinator, and Bookkeeper, even if all those roles are assigned to the same person. A larger organization might spread the financial processes across several roles, including Controller, Accountant,

Customer Onboarding Specialist, Accounts Receivable Manager, Accounts Payable Manager, Expense Coordinator, Cash Manager, and Payroll Coordinator.

Consider roles you will add as you grow

List both current roles in your organization and future roles that you will need when your organization is "full grown" or at its optimal size. You can create an org chart that shows your future organization with all the roles you will need. This will help you plan when and how to fill those new roles.

Consider different types of workers

Remember that roles are not just inside your organization. You can have internal roles filled by employees and external roles filled by contractors and service providers.

Consider your org chart

Look at all the people and titles on your current organizational chart. Ideally, each role should be shown as a separate box on your org chart, as shown below.

Figure 5-2. Role-based Org Chart. Create an org chart with roles, then add names of people.

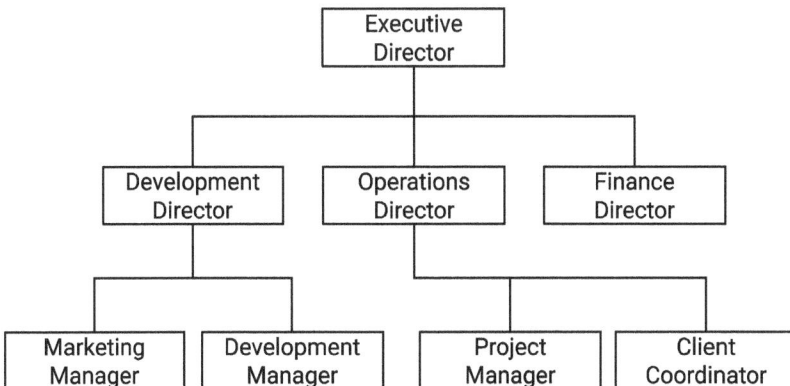

One person can fill multiple boxes. For example, your Director of Administration may also serve as Finance Manager and Human Resources Manager.

How to refine your list of roles

Now that you've created an initial set of roles, let's look at ways to refine your list.

Add a role description

Describe every role with a brief note that explains what it does. Short descriptions will provide a head start when we identify the processes covered by that role.

Unbundle big positions

Positions like Executive Director, Operations Director, and Office Manager can span multiple functional areas. To unbundle a big position, ask, "As we grow, what aspects of this broad role could be delegated to someone else?"

For example, if Maria is the primary person who handles finances for your organization, then "Finance Coordinator" could be a fitting role for her. But you could also think about Maria's work in terms of the multiple, smaller roles that she fills:

- Bookkeeper
- Accounts Payable Coordinator
- Accounts Receivable Coordinator
- Collections Coordinator
- Payroll Coordinator
- Tax Filings Coordinator

Describing Maria's work in terms of multiple roles can help when you need to split her duties with a second person.

At a startup school that I worked with, a single person held the following roles:

- Academic Dean
- Director of Curriculum
- Upper School Teacher

- Director of Upper School
- Senior Trip Coordinator
- Director of College Counseling

That workload was manageable with a few dozen students, but as the school grew, some of those roles were assigned to others to lighten the workload.

Another company I worked with wanted to hire a Chief Operations Officer to oversee all of the firm's client-facing activities. But when that COO position was unbundled, it revealed three large roles:

- Director of Marketing
- Director of Sales
- Director of Client Services

And there were even more roles under each of those roles that the same person would also fill. After seeing how overwhelming that would be for one person, the company's leadership decided to split the duties among multiple people instead of overloading one person.

If someone has duties in different areas of your business, give them a separate role for each area. If your receptionist not only receives visitors but also helps out with website updates, market research, and keeping the kitchen organized, then define four roles: Office Receptionist, Website Editor, Assistant Market Researcher, and Kitchen Coordinator.

Combine tiny roles

One person shouldn't have too many small roles. If two related roles (in the same functional area) are always assigned to the same person, then merge those two roles. In an office setting, the roles of "Coffee Machine Cleaner" and "Refrigerator Restocker" would be too tiny. But "Kitchen Coordinator" or "Office Manager" might be suitable.

Ensure the list of roles is complete

Remember to make the list of roles for your organization mutually exclusive and collectively exhaustive (MECE). Perform a completeness check by asking, "is everything we do covered by the list of roles we've collected?"

Ensure you define roles for everyone who works for and with your organization: employees, external contractors, service providers, volunteers, interns, part-time staff, and temporary workers.

Don't forget to include outsourced roles such as Tax Accountant, Graphic Designer, Ad Agency, Cleaning Service, or Marketing Consultant. These roles may be filled with contractors instead of employees, but they are still vital to your business.

Also, consider unassigned roles and things you should be doing but are not. One company scattered its processes related to safety training and fire drills among multiple people with no clear owner. A better approach is to define the roles of Safety Manager and Fire Drill Coordinator. You can assign specific, verifiable, safety-related duties to these roles.

If you think of roles that would be helpful, but "nobody has time," make a list of those roles. You may be able to assign those roles to a person already doing similar work. Or you can fill those roles after you have freed up time by applying the Process Prescription.

Compare people in the same role

Do all the people assigned to the same role do the same things?

If not, find the "extra" things that some people have been assigned, and label those as additional roles.

For example, one Fourth Grade teacher at a school is assigned extra responsibilities. Unlike the other Fourth Grade teachers, this person coordinates lesson plans and arranges a field trip each semester. You could separate this person's extra duties into a "Lead Teacher" or "Coordinating Teacher" role that is assigned to that one teacher. The teacher then has two roles: Fourth Grade Teacher and Lead Teacher. Or even split this into three roles: Fourth Grade Teacher, Lesson Planner, and Field Trip Coordinator. If that teacher leaves the school, you can reassign the extra roles (and all the related processes) to another Fourth Grade Teacher.

Checklist for identifying roles

To conclude this chapter, here's a summary of how to identify your organization's roles.

- ☐ Identify the people who will serve as your organization's Process Leader, Process Architect, and Process Pilot.
- ☐ Consider each person individually, working to understand all of their roles.
- ☐ Make sure your list of roles is MECE (mutually exclusive, collectively exhaustive). Your list of roles should cover everything your company does. Include roles filled by your contractors, service providers, and vendors.
- ☐ Avoid huge roles. If a person has one role but is responsible for running half the company, then their role is too big. Consider giving them at least one role in each functional area where they work.
- ☐ Avoid tiny roles.

Chapter 6

How to Identify Your Processes

Identify	Describe	Use	Improve
Chapter 4. Identify Your **Functional Areas**		Chapter 10. Use Your Processes in **Day-to-Day Work**	Chapter 13. **Improve** Your Processes
Chapter 5. Identify Your **Roles**	Chapter 8. Describe Your Processes With **Attributes**	Chapter 11. Use Your Processes With **Your Team**	Chapter 14. Improve Your Processes by **Learning from Others**
Chapter 6. Identify Your **Processes**	Chapter 9. Describe Your Processes Using **How-To Guides**	Chapter 12. Use Your Processes With **Business Frameworks**	Chapter 15. Improve Your Processes Using **External Resources**
Chapter 7. Identify **Gaps and Opportunities**			

Now that you have created your lists of functional areas and roles, it's time to identify specific processes under each area and role.

We will build a Process Library, which is a valuable repository of your knowledge and How-to Guides.

Remember that we've defined a process as a sequence of steps that results in a desired outcome. A process can either be 1) a scheduled, recurring event or 2) an action performed only as-needed.

In this chapter, we'll explore how to spot the different types of processes in all the areas of your organization.

Why you need to identify all your processes

Someone may say, "We need to focus on just a few urgent processes. We don't need to take a full inventory of our processes."

If you don't identify all your processes, how do you know what processes are missing? In other words, what processes *should* you have but don't have? Your missing processes may not be required for survival, but they may be required for growth. Your current processes may keep you alive, but do they allow you to thrive?

Suppose your company wants more sales. You could just focus on the single process, "How to generate new inquiries," which includes buying ads and refining your prospecting techniques. But this tunnel vision could be short-sighted. Getting more sales is based on a collection of related processes across your whole organization: production, marketing, customer service, and finance. All of these affect your ability to sell more.

Selling more requires a solid "business operating system" with many refined processes, not just a single "How to generate new inquiries" process. It would be best if you understood how your processes relate to each other. For example, "How to generate new inquiries" feeds into "How to follow up with an inquiry," which leads to "How to close the sale," which results in "How to onboard a new customer." Even if your process for "How to generate new inquiries" is working fine, you need to evaluate the entire sales flow to ensure the foundational marketing processes are in place. When you identify all your processes, you can uncover gaps and opportunities. Perhaps you're missing a process for creating a marketing strategy or a process for scheduling your monthly marketing activities.

Also, there could be several processes that need work before you can generate new inquiries, such as the following:

- How to develop credibility in your industry (e.g., through articles, books, and speaking engagements)
- How to hire the right marketing team members
- How to develop a plan for content marketing
- How to create an understandable market strategy
- How to nurture existing customers
- How to develop a referral network

You can't view a process in a vacuum. You need to identify all your processes to see which processes are missing, incomplete, overlapping, redundant, or unneeded.

How to focus your attention by identifying your processes

Other projects and priorities may seem more urgent than organizing and improving your processes. You have unfinished tasks that are due soon. You have people insisting that their "one thing" is what your business needs to focus on. They say, "It's not all about process; it's *really* about something else."

The Process Prescription helps you evaluate competing priorities and focus your effort on the right areas. Let's look at some of these competing priorities and ask some clarifying questions.

"It's all about **cash flow**. Without cash, our business will starve." True! But how do you monitor and optimize cash flow? Which processes affect your cash flow most directly?

"It's all about **hiring the right people**. Systems without people to run them are meaningless." That is 100% correct. But how do you find and keep the best people? How can you do this better than your competitors? What processes do you need to keep your team engaged and enthusiastic about their work?

"It's all about setting and achieving the **right objectives**. We'll never get there if we don't know where we're going" Affirmative. But how do you set, manage, track, and reset your objectives? How do you provide feedback on individual and group objectives? How do you adjust objectives mid-course when things change?

"It's all about having **the right product or solution**. We can't sell garbage. Great products sell themselves." Good point. But how do you innovate? How do you refine an existing product? How do you determine the preferences of your customers? How do you move from idea to reality? How do you test a new idea?

"It's all about our **clients' needs**. We don't have a real business if we're not meeting a need." Yes, but how do you assess your client's needs? How often? How do you use the information you collect? How do you translate a client need into sustained revenue?

"It's all about **sales**! Without revenue, our business isn't sustainable." Agreed. How do your most successful salespeople sell? How do you maximize your best sales channels? What's the best source of new revenue? How do you prioritize and qualify sales prospects? How do you set, manage, track, and reset sales targets? How do you learn from sales successes and sales failures?

"It's all about **marketing**! Leads and new prospects are the lifeblood of our business." Yes, and how do you market? How do you choose the right channels? How do you find what's working and what's not? How do you calculate your return on marketing investment?

The theme here is that your business is a complex organism with interrelated parts. While each area does need attention, it's not **all** about any one particular area. Saint Paul explained it this way, "But now there are many members, but one body. And the eye cannot say to the hand, 'I have no need of you'; or again the head to the feet, 'I have no need of you.' On the contrary, it is much truer that the members of the body which seem to be weaker are necessary."[1]

Your body is a collection of systems, such as the respiratory, circulatory, and digestive systems. You need all those systems to work well together. A physical exam by a doctor looks at all the systems and isolates any problems. Likewise, your business is a collection of processes within functional areas.

The Process Prescription looks at all your processes to identify what's working well and what needs improvement.

Your business's success depends on your systems working together. Use the Process Prescription to increase your focus on the areas that need the most attention and develop a system to continuously improve your processes.

How to find your organization's processes

Now let's look at how we can discover the processes inside your organization. To help identify all your processes systematically, we'll investigate four topics:

1. Ground Rules - How to collect and name your processes.
2. Nouns and Verbs - How to find everything affected by your processes.
3. Role Interviews - How to gather process information from the people who know best.
4. Process Library - How to store and organize your process information.

Ground Rules

Before we dive into the Identify step, let's establish a few standards to guide our work.

Name your processes using "how to"

Each process we identify will be a verb phrase, such as "run payroll" or "send the monthly marketing newsletter."

If we apply "How to" as a prefix for each process, it's easy to remember to use a verb phrase to name your process. Using that pattern, here are some example processes:

- How to run payroll
- How to perform the weekly marketing tasks
- How to create the board meeting packet
- How to conduct the monthly safety meeting

Each verb after "How to" in the above list has a noun (payroll, tasks, packet, and meeting) as its direct object. This direct object indicates what the verb relates to, applies to, or acts on.

It's tempting to use just adjectives and nouns (such as "monthly accounting" or "network management") to name a process, but using the formula of "how to + verb + noun" is better. "How to + verb + noun" provides more description and a clearer understanding of what a process does. For example, "How to run the monthly accounting cycle" is more descriptive than "Monthly Accounting."

Figure 6-1. Naming Processes. Provide enough description in a process name.

Process names that are too short (using only adjective + noun)	Process names that have better descriptions (using 'how to' + verb + noun)
financial close	how to close the monthly books and create financial reports
inspections checklist	how to inspect house while under construction
prospecting methods	how to qualify a prospective customer
customer financing	how to help a customer finance their purchase
warranty claims	how to provide warranty services to clients

Another type of problem occurs if you combine an ambiguous verb (such as manage, run, or administer) with a broad, ambiguous noun (such as accounting, culture, or management). You risk creating a process that is too big to define accurately.

For example, "How to manage the monthly accounting routine" might be fine for a solopreneur or micro-business. But if you have multiple people in your accounting department, you'll need a more granular list of processes that you divide among multiple roles.

You can use the verb "manage" if you have a lot of small tasks that are completed together, and you don't need to break them all out separately.

For example, a company might have the process "How to manage accounts payable," which is a collection of tasks that are performed weekly to pay the bills. Don't overuse "manage" if you can use a more precise verb, such as "How to pay bills."

Name your processes using a pattern

Use the "How-to" prefix to enforce a verb being a part of every process name.

Here are a few patterns you can use to create process names, with an example for each.

Pattern 1: How to + *verb* + *noun* + by doing ...

> How to prioritize product ideas by conducting a customer survey

Pattern 2: How to + *verb* + *noun* + using ...

> How to update a customer profile using our CRM software

Pattern 3: How to + *verb* + adjective + *noun* + using ...

> How to create the income statement using our accounting software

Pattern 4: How to + *verb* from *noun 1* to *noun 2*.

> How to convert an inquiry from a prospect to a customer

Pattern 5: How to + *verb* + *noun 1* for *noun 2*.

> How to conduct training for new team members

Pattern 6: How to + *verb* + *noun* + frequency

> How to file taxes quarterly

Match each process to a role, not a team

A process named "How to test the software" could be assigned to your Quality Assurance team, but a better breakout would be a collection of smaller processes that are assigned to individuals instead of the entire team. For example, here's a set of smaller processes related to testing:

- How to run bench tests
- How to run a stress test for a new release
- How to review test results
- How to create an issue in the bug-tracking system
- How to conduct a final acceptance test with the customer

Don't worry about nomenclature

The people being interviewed about their processes may refer to systems, routines, procedures, tasks, steps, checkpoints, and to-dos. Don't attempt to change the terms they use or how they describe their processes. Capture whatever they say and pay attention to the verbs and nouns they use. We are still in the Identify step of the Process Prescription, so it's not time to make big changes. We will refine the process details later.

Choose processes that are not too big or small

Any unit of work that is done repeatedly should be described by a process. But how fine-grained should you get with your processes? How many processes should you identify? How big should a process be?

Does a process require many people with lots of collaboration over a long period of time? If so, break that process down into smaller processes that are completed in sequence. Call the larger process "how to lead this" or "how to manage that" and then describe that high-level process with smaller, supporting processes.

Let's look at marketing as an example. "How to do marketing" is definitely a process, but it's too broad if you have multiple marketing channels and multiple people working on your marketing processes.

If your marketing and lead generation process is simple, you could consider having a single marketing process, such as "how to generate new leads and find prospective customers." Creating a single, broad process like that will prevent you from scheduling or assigning separate marketing processes. A better method is to define distinct, repeatable processes organized into subareas. Here's an example of how that might look.

- Outbound marketing
    ◦ How to host an event
    ◦ How to ask for a referral
    ◦ How to manage Facebook advertising
- Inbound marketing
    ◦ How to manage social media
    ◦ How to post an article on the website
- Marketing support
    ◦ How to create the weekly marketing dashboard
    ◦ How to update the website

A larger company could further divide "How to update the website" so that multiple people can work on separate processes, such as the following:

- How to update product information
- How to add a new blog post
- How to create and schedule social media posts
- How to add a new website section
- How to add a new event
- How to add and remove products

Avoid creating processes that are too small. For example, "How to check the number of subscribers on our mailing list" should be part of "How to create the weekly marketing dashboard." "How to change the font color for a headline on the website" should be part of "How to update the website."

If "How to manage finances" is too broad, break the Finance area into subareas such as Order-to-Cash, Procure-to-Pay, and Record-to-Report. Then identify smaller processes under each of those subareas.

If "How to maintain the company facilities" is too broad, you could create smaller processes based on systems and locations, such as the following:

- How to manage the company IT network
- How to maintain the HVAC at the Jones Road warehouse
- How to manage the janitorial services vendor

You can split or combine processes in the future if needed. Just get started with identifying your processes and see how it goes.

To define processes that are not too small and not too big, make sure each process meets these three criteria:

1. The process is owned by one role. This means that the process is completed by a person in that role, or a person in that role is responsible for seeing that the process is completed.

2. The process is understandable and completable. Some processes can be completed in one session or sitting, others may span multiple days. The person running the process should be able to tell when they've completed it. If a process is continuous, the person should know when they've completed one iteration or cycle of the process.

3. The process is defined by inputs and outputs. You need to know what's needed to start the process and what successful completion looks like. A process should result in a completed transaction, event, or output.

Nouns and Verbs

You can create a list of processes by thinking about what your organization does in terms of verbs and nouns.

Identify processes by looking for nouns and verbs

You can list all the nouns you work with in categories such as people, places, things, products, and projects. Then you can identify all the verbs that apply to each noun, such as create, update, review, remove, start, stop, and test. This provides a way to create verb + noun pairs that describe your processes.

Start with lists of nouns you can observe within your organization. Create a list of verbs based on how you interact with each noun. For example, if the noun is "Injection Molding Machine" (from your list of equipment), ask verb-related questions about that noun:

•   Who runs it?

- How do they start it?
- How do they run it?
- How do they stop it?
- How do they reset it?
- How do they clean it?
- How do they maintain it?
- How do they troubleshoot it?
- How do they repair it?

Each of these verb-noun pairs could become a process. If several related verbs occur in sequence, you can create processes that include multiple steps. For example, "How to operate the Injection Molding Machine" could include how to start, run, stop, reset, and clean the machine. But "How to perform preventative maintenance on the Injection Molding Machine" could be a separate process since it's done at a different time by a different person.

This "verb plus noun" approach was used to put Neil Armstrong and eventually 11 other humans on the moon. NASA's Apollo Guidance Computer (AGC) had 78 kilobytes of memory, which is minuscule by today's standards. The AGC did not even have a QWERTY keyboard or a screen. It simply had a number pad, a few extra buttons, ten warning lights, and three output rows where numbers could be displayed. It looked like a fancy calculator.

Despite its limitations, this computer was versatile. The versatility stemmed from a "verb plus noun" method of issuing instructions to the AGC. The astronauts could enter a two-digit command (a number from 01 to 99) that represented a verb. Then they could enter a second two-digit command that represented a noun. This allowed the crew to perform hundreds of essential tasks. For example, entering Verb 50 meant "PLEASE PERFORM," and Noun 18 meant "AUTO MNVR TO FDAI RPY ANGLES (0.01°)." Combining the verb and noun and translating to English reveals the intended command: "Please perform the automatic maneuvering to the flight director attitude indicator with roll, pitch, and yaw angles expressed as multiples of 0.01 degrees." [2]

The flexible "verb plus noun" instruction format allowed the astronauts to run all the AGC processes that got them to the moon and back.

Make lists of nouns

First, let's look at nouns since they're usually easier to identify than verbs.

You've already identified your organization's functional areas and roles, but what about the other collections of things you need to run your business? Start by making three lists of nouns:

- **Software and Online Resources**: What applications do you use? This includes software-as-a-service (SaaS) apps, locally installed apps, mobile apps, online forms, websites, and databases. Your accounting system may have a list of your software subscriptions.

- **Events**: What scheduled events does your organization host? What activities do your people attend? What happens daily, weekly, monthly, quarterly, and yearly? This includes meetings, conferences, presentations, webinars, training sessions, orientations, inspections, audits, and parties. Expand this list to include any recurring activity.

- **Other Companies**: What other organizations do you interact with? This includes customers, service providers, suppliers, vendors, partners, affiliates, associations, and government agencies.

Now make more lists of nouns to round out all the other areas of your business:

- **People**: employees, contractors, volunteers, consultants, owners / shareholders, customers, prospective hires, prospective customers, industry leaders, committee members, advisors, donors, board members, service providers

- **Places**: offices, plants, factories, campuses, remote locations, temporary locations

- **Things**: equipment, machinery, computers, tools, vehicles, supplies, raw materials, work-in-progress, finished products, printed materials, promotional materials

- **Information**: forms, reports, files, government filings, receipts, invoices, how-to guides, policies, inquiries, surveys, requests, proposals, mailing lists, leases, agreements, contracts, notes, meeting minutes, courses, manuals, video, audio, photos, documents, spreadsheets, folders, diagrams, tables, charts, dashboards, metrics, templates

If the nouns are too many to digest at one time, focus your thinking on just one functional area. For example, what nouns are required to perform our Finance function? This would likely include your financial accounting software, computers, reports, finance team members, and customers. You can exclude things that are not directly related to accounting processes, such as machinery, marketing events, and furniture.

Focus on just one role at a time. During your role interviews, you can ask, "what is all the stuff you work with?" That question will identify nouns.

You can also focus on just one type of noun. For example, list all the different types of customers you have. You don't need to list your customers individually, but you should consider their differences that require specialized activities.

Add verbs to the nouns

Now we can identify the verbs that apply to these nouns, which can also reveal processes that we haven't thought of until now. Remember the "Make, Market, Manage" framework we used to find functional areas? We can also consider verbs in these three categories. Below are some verbs that may help you identify some of your existing processes. Add a verb to each of your nouns and use a pattern from earlier in this chapter to create a process name. Scan this list of verbs to see if any other verb-noun pairs come to mind.

Figure 6-2. Process Verbs. Review this list of verbs to help identify current or missing processes.

"Make" verbs	"Market" verbs	"Manage" verbs
add, assemble, assist, complete, conduct, create, cultivate, decide, define, deliver, develop, do, document, drop, establish, estimate, finalize, generate, handle, help, integrate, issue, log, mail, make, manufacture, open, operate, order, package, perform, plan, post, prepare, process, produce, program, provide, pull, purchase, push, receive, release, repair, script, send, set, setup, sign, start, take, transport, use, work with, write	administer, advertise, answer, arrange, assign, attend, award, communicate, conduct, coordinate, counsel, email, enlist, facilitate, follow-up, manage, meet, notify, participate in, present, publicize, publish, recruit, remind, reply, report, reserve, respond to, script, sell, submit, survey, update, write	archive, assess, audit, backup, bid, bill, budget, capture, charge, check, choose, clean, clean up, close, close-out, collect, curate, enroll, evaluate, file, find, fix, format, gather, get, give, hire, inspect, interview, maintain, measure, monitor, nurture, observe, offboard, onboard, organize, pay, prioritize, record, refine, resolve, review, revise, run, schedule, score, store, tear down, track, troubleshoot, validate, unenroll, verify, withdraw

A few caveats about this list of verbs:

- It's not comprehensive, so add other verbs based on how your business works.
- It's meant to stimulate your thinking, so use synonyms as needed.
- It includes some verbs that can apply in multiple areas.
- It's not MECE. It contains several synonyms, so pick your favorites.

Identify processes using existing job descriptions

If you have existing job descriptions or position descriptions, use those as a starting point. Isolate all the "verb plus noun" pairs mentioned in the job description. If some descriptions are vague, use your knowledge of that position to list additional "verb plus noun" pairs that add specific details about what that job involves. Extract all the nouns from the job description and add the appropriate verbs.

Identify processes using existing documents

Gather existing documents that describe what your company does and who does it. Look for processes using the following:

- Your existing org chart. This was useful for identifying roles, and it can also remind you of processes that are run by each person or position on the chart.
- An employee roster with job titles. Pull this from your HR system.
- Your annual budget. Since this shows every revenue and expense category, you can ensure you're not leaving anything out.
- Your Chart of Accounts from your accounting software can remind you of processes related to revenue, expenses, assets, and liabilities.
- Your existing documentation for how to complete tasks.
- Your marketing materials. Because you already describe "what you do" on your website and brochures, these resources may help identify your customer-facing processes.

Identify processes by looking for pathways

You can look for journeys, pathways, and "value streams" within your business. These occur when you combine a sequence of activities to produce the desired output. A pathway can involve multiple processes and span multiple functional areas, such as converting a customer order into cash-in-the-bank.

These pathways follow the pattern "we need to convert A into B." For example,

- A law firm needs to convert an initial inquiry into a client paying a retainer.
- An online retailer needs to convert a website visitor to a repeat customer.
- A church needs to convert a first-time guest into an active member.
- A school needs to convert an open house visitor into an enrolled student.
- A non-profit's development officer needs to convert a sympathetic community member into a donor.

Pathways can also describe how and where your organization adds value.

- A manufacturer needs to convert raw materials into a finished product.
- A real estate investor needs to convert a dilapidated property into a move-in-ready home.
- A software company needs to convert a new user into a power user who is a raving fan.
- A cleaning company needs to convert a dirty building into a clean building.

Each of these pathways can become one or more processes. If some of these pathways are too broad, you can break them down into smaller processes that each have a beginning and end.

Identify processes by considering process frequencies

List everything you do on a recurring basis, from daily to annually. Consider recurring processes in each functional area. For example, recurring processes in the finance area include budgeting, reporting, and government filings. A recurring leadership process might be "How to plan the annual executive retreat." You may also have processes for conducting board meetings and updating the board calendar.

Identify processes related to your annual cycles. These cycles can include the fiscal year, a busy season, holidays, the calendar year, the school year, or a contract year. Schools run many annual processes: onboarding new teachers, archiving data, preparing facilities, and updating handbooks.

Consider grouping related daily activities into a single checklist that can be run by the person in the assigned role.

Identify processes using a month-by-month grid

To help identify some of your less-frequent processes, you can create a grid showing the 12 months as rows and your functional areas as columns.

Figure 6-3. Monthly Process Grid. Fill in this grid by asking, "What processes do we run each month in each functional area?"

	Functional Areas					
	Finance	Admin & Infra	Marketing	Sales	HR	Services
Jan						
Feb						
Mar						
Apr						
May						
Jun						
Jul						
Aug						
Sep						
Oct						
Nov						
Dec						

For each month and area, ask, "What do we do in that month for that area?"

Capture your unscheduled processes

Even if something happens rarely, it needs a process. Some of these infrequent events fall into the "not if, but when" category. For example, your organization's leadership will eventually retire or leave the business. You should have a succession plan for when that happens. Here are some other unexpected or infrequent things that could benefit from a defined process:

- How to prepare for an extreme weather event
- How to survive a power outage
- How to deal with an unexpected absence
- How to replace a vendor or service provider
- How to resolve a supply shortage
- How to respond to a data breach

This collection of processes can form your organization's business continuity plan. You can decide how much detail and effort to put into each of these based on the likelihood of each event's occurrence and your potential for loss.

There could also be once-in-a-career events such as mergers, acquisitions, or company dissolution. These type of rare event requires specialist knowledge, you should at least know who to contact when you need guidance or how to get a referral to an appropriate advisor.

Role Interviews

Now you can use your established ground rules and list of nouns to conduct face-to-face interviews with each person who is assigned a role. These interviews are a vital part of process discovery, since the people running the processes know them best.

Interview people by role

To find the processes for each role in your organization, start with one person and ask them about one of the roles they fill:

- "What do you do in your role as __?"

Write down everything they say that they do to fulfill that role. Focus on one role at a time. Repeat this for each of that person's roles. This is the essence of process identification: finding the activities for each role.

If multiple people have the same role, interview two or three people in that role and combine their answers. If you discover a lot of variation in the answers from people in the same role, conduct more interviews until you have discovered everything that role covers.

At this point, we are trying to capture the *names* of the processes under each role, not all of the process details. If an interviewee provides a few details about how a process works, that's fine, but don't attempt to record every step of every process. We'll look at how to describe each process in more detail in Chapters 8 and 9.

A single one-hour session or a couple of half-hour sessions could be enough time to identify all the processes for someone's roles.

Who should you interview first? Here are a few options for getting started with role interviews.

- Start with yourself. You know your own roles, activities, and routines. For each of your roles, list everything you do. Compare the lists for each role. Are there similar processes among your roles? Did you miss anything? Do you need to add a process for Role A based on what you do in Role B?
- Start with someone on your team or someone who reports to you. Since you already have some idea about their work and their output, you can ask insightful questions to identify their processes.
- Start with a peer who has a role similar to yours. As you learn what they do, you may think of similar processes that apply to your roles.
- Start with someone who has been with your organization for a long time. They can identify rare or unusual processes in addition to regular, recurring processes.
- Start with someone who is new to your organization. Have them identify their roles and capture all the related processes. They can jot down notes and questions as they learn.
- Start with someone who is eager to learn and improve. Find someone who has the willingness and vision to analyze what they do and capture their processes. Make a note of how they follow the Process Prescription.

Once you've completed a role-by-role interview for one person, write down your interview process. Note how you resolve any questions from the interviewee. Repeat your interview process with more people. Find ways to make role interviews easy for both the interviewer and the interviewee. For example,

- List processes as you identify them on a shared document or whiteboard. This view of everything may spark more ideas and allow for real-time clarifications.

- Remind the interviewee that forgotten or overlooked processes can be added later. The interview is meant to create a "first draft" of the processes for each role.
- Find a comfortable time and location for the interview.
- Pick an appropriate interview length. In my experience, most individual interviews can be completed in 60 minutes or less. A rule of thumb: don't exceed one hour for a single interview session. Schedule a follow-up session if more time is needed for someone with multiple roles.

Use an interview guide

For each role you've identified, ask the person in that role to answer a set of written questions. Use the list of questions below to develop an interview guide that works best for your organization.

What?

- What areas are your responsibility?
- What things do you create in this role? (e.g., documents, products, outputs)
- What are the processes that create those outputs?
- What are the things you do for others? (e.g., submit approvals, provide services, fulfill requests)
- What are the inputs (such as requests, materials, supplies, prerequisites, approvals, and resources) you need for this role?
- What are all the "nouns" that are a part of this role?
- What are the key metrics and things you track? How do you track those?

When?

- When do you work on recurring tasks?
- When are your scheduled events? Consider meetings you attend, reports you create, things you approve, and things you submit to others.

How?

- Do you use existing process documentation?
- How is your job performance measured?

Who?

- Who do you interact with inside your organization?
- Who do you interact with outside your organization? Consider customers, suppliers, contractors, service providers, and partners.

Conduct a workshop

If some people in your organization are familiar with a wide range of processes, you can conduct a process discovery workshop by facilitating a group interview. This group can list the corresponding processes for each functional area, subarea, and role. The participants can respond to each other's input and verify more details than would be possible with one-on-one interviews. Break up the workshop into sessions of 90 minutes or less.

The workshop should focus on identifying processes, not describing them in detail. Resist the temptation to delve into how each process works since that would require too much time at this stage. Do collect any quick descriptions about how a process works or what needs attention later.

Process Library

As you identify your organization's processes, use your Process Library as a holding tank to keep track of them all. Use your Process Library to prioritize what can be improved to make the biggest impact.

How to create a Process Library

You can start to build your Process Library at a list in a document or spreadsheet. Create one row for each process. Include these columns for each process: functional area, subarea (if needed), the assignee's role, and the process name. As your Process Library grows, you can use process management software and document management tools to organize your processes.

Your Process Library should start to look like the example in Figure 6-4.

Figure 6-4. Basic Process Library. Organize the details about each of your processes to form a Process Library.

Area	Role	Process Name
Finance	Accounting Manager	how to create reports for leadership meeting
Finance	Bookkeeper	how to close the books at month-end
Finance	Bookkeeper	how to reconcile bank account
Finance	Bookkeeper	how to process expense reports
Marketing	Content Manager	how to add a new blog post

How to triage your processes

Step 1 of the Process Prescription (Identify) aims to capture all your processes before focusing on improvement opportunities. If you're facing an urgent problem or process emergency, triage your list of processes and fix the ones that need immediate attention. Here are some ways to prioritize your processes.

- By person. If you know that a key person will leave (or could leave), focus on capturing that person's processes.
- By department. If one department is performing poorly and affecting the rest of your organization, focus on that department's processes first.
- By consistency. If one person runs a process really well, but another person runs the same process poorly, flag that process for a closer look.
- By opportunity. Pinpoint where you're seeing progress, but want better results. What is frustrating you? Focus on improving those areas with the highest potential.
- By risk. What is the highest risk? Which process would cause the most problems if it failed?

Checklist for identifying processes

- ☐ Consider each person and each role in your organization. Find every process for one role, then move to the next role.
- ☐ Start each process name with "How to..."
- ☐ Don't make a process too big or small.
- ☐ Create a Process Library that lists your processes.
- ☐ Triage and prioritize your processes if needed.

Chapter 7

How to Identify Gaps and Opportunities

Identify	Describe	Use	Improve
Chapter 4. Identify Your **Functional Areas**		Chapter 10. Use Your Processes in **Day-to-Day Work**	Chapter 13. **Improve** Your Processes
Chapter 5. Identify Your **Roles**	Chapter 8. Describe Your Processes With **Attributes**	Chapter 11. Use Your Processes With **Your Team**	Chapter 14. Improve Your Processes by **Learning from Others**
Chapter 6. Identify Your **Processes**	Chapter 9. Describe Your Processes Using **How-To Guides**	Chapter 12. Use Your Processes With **Business Frameworks**	Chapter 15. Improve Your Processes Using **External Resources**
Chapter 7. Identify **Gaps and Opportunities**			

Early in my career, I was a consultant at Arthur D. Little, the international management consultancy founded in 1886. Despite being an old company, they were willing to try new things. While I was there, the company launched an initiative called TQM, which stands for Total Quality Management. The senior leadership was committed to getting buy-in from everyone. The head of the company visited our branch office in Houston to impress upon us the importance of this strategic effort. We were divided into teams and left to decide what we wanted to improve. We could choose to work on whatever TQM initiative we dreamed up. My group, not wanting to fail, picked something easy: how to standardize the abbreviations that we used in our reports. This was indeed an area of need and had some value. But was it the best use of our time? Was it the best way for us to improve the business? Did it really matter if we abbreviated "thousand cubic feet" as MCF or Mcf? Probably not.

Operationally, we were diligent. Strategically, we were ignorant. We chose to work on something that was inconsequential to the firm's success.

How do we identify missing processes that can improve our strategic thinking? We don't want to become more efficient while headed in the wrong direction. A friend who runs a commercial real estate brokerage posed the question, "How do I turn strategic thinking into processes that improve my business? For example, what are the processes for business planning and strengthening our company's culture?"

These questions cut to the heart of the matter. What's the best way to define processes that require high-level, abstract thinking and then affect the entire business? You could create one "How to develop strategy" process that covers your whole organization. A more thorough approach would be to apply strategy to every functional area. Finance needs strategy, but so does marketing, and don't forget about your hiring and training strategy.

How to apply four levels of focus

So far, we've identified processes using roles, nouns, and verbs. Now let's add another parameter that can help us identify processes: the level of strategic focus.

We can identify processes in each functional area using four levels, getting more specific with each level.

1. Strategy. At this highest level, you create processes to achieve strategic objectives that will lead to long-term success. These objectives typically have a time horizon beyond one year. An example of a Strategy process is "How to create and update the 5-year Strategic Financial Plan."

2. Planning. Processes at this level define the 'who' 'when' and 'how much' for the processes in a functional area. This includes creating plans with specific tasks, assignments, and timelines. These processes typically have a time horizon related to the upcoming year or quarter. An example of a Planning process is "How to update and finalize the annual budget."

3. Analysis. These processes help you understand what's happening for the purpose of directing or correcting. These processes ingest data, extract insights, and then feed information to other processes. An example of an Analysis process is "How to run and review the monthly variance report."

4. Operations. These processes are for doing the day-to-day work. The bulk of an organization's time will be spent at this level. An example of an Operations process is "How to pay bills and invoices."

Each functional area should have at least one process in each of the four levels. My TQM experience would have benefited from more thinking about strategy, planning, and analysis before we dove into the operational details of standardizing abbreviations.

This four-tier Strategy-Planning-Analysis-Operations approach is similar to the one used by information technology consultants at Arthur D. Little to create an Information Supply Matrix. Using this approach, consultants identify processes at each focus level and create a poster showing all of an organization's processes. Each process is color-coded based on the availability of information needed to run the process.

- Green means that enough information is available to run the process effectively.
- Yellow means that more information is needed.
- Red means that the process can't run due to a lack of information.

Once this triage is done, the consultants can help the client fix their information supply problems.

We can apply this approach to create a Process Matrix, which allows us to see if we're missing processes in any of the four focus areas.

How to create a Process Matrix

A Process Matrix is a way to visualize the four focus areas and all your functional areas on one page. The Process Matrix is a grid listing the processes in your Process Library. You can see gaps and refine your list of processes using this single view.

To create a Process Matrix, use your functional areas as columns and the four strategic focus levels as rows. Figure 7-1 shows an example Process Matrix for a service company.

Figure 7-1. Process Matrix. Create a Process Matrix to find gaps in your process coverage.

		Functional areas					
		Finance	Admin & Infra	Marketing	Sales	HR	Services
Focus areas	Strategy						
	Planning						
	Analysis						
	Operations						

You can list process names in each cell of the matrix.

Use the rows and columns of the grid to identify missing processes. Each cell in the matrix should have at least one process. For example, if the cell at the intersection of the Human Resources column and the Strategy row is empty, ask yourself strategic HR questions, such as "What should we be doing now to prepare for our hiring needs over the next several years?"

Once you've identified a gap, identify processes to fill the gap.

Let's continue using HR as an example and ask a few more questions based on each focus area. This will help identify processes along the different planning horizons of your business.

- HR Strategy questions that focus on preparing for the years ahead
  - What is our 5-year strategic hiring plan?
  - How do we evaluate our compensation policies and benefits?
  - What skills will be needed in the coming years? How will we acquire those skills?
  - What are our long-term objectives for taking care of our team members?
  - How do people grow with our organization during their careers?
- HR Planning questions that focus on the next 12 months
  - How do we create and review quarterly Objectives and Key Results (OKRs)?
  - How do we schedule regular feedback sessions for our team members?
  - How do we create and update our annual professional development calendar?
- HR Analysis questions that focus on reporting, monitoring, and optimizing
  - How do we collect meaningful HR data?
  - How do we use that data to improve?
  - How do we assess the effectiveness of our training?
- HR Operations questions that focus on doing the day-to-day work
  - How do we capture ideas and suggestions from our team members?
  - How do we recognize and reward people?
  - How do we attend a professional development event or class?

How to find gaps using the Process Matrix

Print your Process Matrix on a large page to see all your existing processes in one view. You can look at each functional area separately if you have too many processes to fit on one page. Then do the following:

- Inspect an entire business function (e.g., Finance) by scanning down that column in the Process Matrix. Are you paying attention to all aspects of Finance, from high-level Strategy down to day-to-day Operations? Do the listed processes accurately describe the whole functional area?

- Evaluate a focus area (e.g., Strategy) by scanning across that row in the Process Matrix. Are you being strategic in all areas of your business? Are you considering the long-term implications of what you are doing (or not doing)?

- Find gaps. Where should a process be added?

- Find overlap. Which processes should be merged or moved? Are any processes duplicated or included in more than one functional area? Do any processes need to be combined for simplicity or because one person runs them all in one session?

Add any missing processes to your Process Library based on the information gathered during this review.

Checklist for identifying process gaps and opportunities

- ☐ Include at least one process for Strategy, Planning, Analysis, and Operations in each functional area.
- ☐ Include all the processes you've been "meaning to do" but haven't found the time yet.
- ☐ Include all the processes you've forgotten to do in the past.

Chapter 8

How to Describe Your Processes With Attributes

Identify	Describe	Use	Improve
Chapter 4. Identify Your **Functional Areas**		Chapter 10. Use Your Processes in **Day-to-Day Work**	Chapter 13. **Improve** Your Processes
Chapter 5. Identify Your **Roles**	Chapter 8. Describe Your Processes With **Attributes**	Chapter 11. Use Your Processes With **Your Team**	Chapter 14. Improve Your Processes by **Learning from Others**
Chapter 6. Identify Your **Processes**	Chapter 9. Describe Your Processes Using **How-To Guides**	Chapter 12. Use Your Processes With **Business Frameworks**	Chapter 15. Improve Your Processes Using **External Resources**
Chapter 7. Identify **Gaps and Opportunities**			

This chapter covers how to describe your processes with useful details. For example,

- Who runs this process?
- What should this process accomplish?
- When should this process be run?
- Where does this process run?
- Why should we run this process?
- How do we run this process?
- How much does this process affect our business?

You can use these additional descriptors to assign, prioritize, and organize your processes. You can sort and triage your processes before creating How-to Guides to document the processes. We'll cover How-to Guides in the next chapter.

Consider how a public library categorizes and sorts its books for easy reference. The library collects useful data about each book: title, author, publisher, publication date, card catalog number, and subject. Since these data elements describe other data (the contents of the book), we sometimes call these descriptive items "metadata," which means "data about the data."

Once you've described your processes with attributes, you can search for processes quickly using a keyword, category, or any other attribute you define. Each process you've identified should already have a functional area, an assigned role, and a process name. You can collect these process descriptions in a spreadsheet or process management software.

Now let's add more attributes to your Process Library including process ID and schedule. Also, add additional information you've captured for each process, such as subarea, focus area, and a brief description.

Your expanded Process Library can look like the example in Figure 8-1.

Figure 8-1. Expanded Process Library. Add attributes for each process to create an expanded Process Library.

Process ID	Functional Area	Subarea	Focus Area	Role	Process Name
FI02	Finance	Reporting	Analysis	Accounting Manager	how to create reports for leadership meeting
FI01	Finance	Bookkeeping	Operations	Bookkeeper	how to close the books at month-end
FI03	Finance	Bookkeeping	Operations	Bookkeeper	how to reconcile bank account
FI04	Finance	A/P	Operations	Bookkeeper	how to process expense reports
MK02	Marketing	Content	Operations	Content Manager	how to add a new blog post

Don't get bogged down trying to add every attribute for every process at this stage. Once you've begun to use your processes, you can add more attributes based on the information you need to prioritize and improve them.

How to create Process IDs

Add a short, unique Process ID to each process, so you can refer to any process using a precise code such as "FI21." Each process will also have a full name, such as "How to run payroll," but the Process ID is a useful nickname.

To create a Process ID naming scheme, create a two-letter abbreviation for each of your functional areas. For example, here are the functional areas of a private school:

- Finance = FI
- Facilities = FA
- Marketing = MA
- Academics = AC
- Governance = GO
- Staffing = ST

Next, assign a unique number to every process in each functional area. Start with 01 and continue until 99. Within a functional area, it doesn't matter which process is 01, 02, or 03. Combine the two-letter area with the two-digit number to create a unique id for every process. For example,

- MA01: How to update the website for a new school year
- MA02: How to prepare and send the monthly newsletter
- ST01: How to onboard a new teacher
- ST02: How to conduct annual teacher training
- FI21: How to run payroll
- FI22: How to prepare the annual budget

Add the Process ID as a prefix when you name your process. The full name of the process could be "FI21: How to run payroll." You can now refer to that exact process using the quick reference "FI21."

You can make your naming scheme more advanced if needed.

- Add a company prefix. If your organization's name starts with the letter D, you could use DFI21 instead of FI21. This is helpful if you access Process Libraries for multiple organizations. If you work with financial processes for both Davidson Industries and Quality Innovations Inc., you can refer to DFI21 and QFI21 and not have two processes using the same 'FI21' ID.
- Add more digits. If you know you'll have more than 100 processes in a functional area, you can add a third digit to the Process ID if you want FI099 to sort before FI100.
- Add subareas. If you have a lot of onboarding processes, you could add a subarea for Onboarding (ON) under Staffing (ST), thereby creating a multi-part ID such as ST-ON-01.

Ensure that your Process IDs don't become too long and unwieldy. It's easier to refer to a process as FI21 instead of DFI-PA-021.

How to add a schedule to a process

When you identified a process, you may have noted if the process recurs on a schedule. Now it's time to add a frequency attribute to every process to formalize that schedule. For each process you've identified, ask "Is this scheduled?"

- If yes, assign a frequency of "Scheduled."
- If no, assign a frequency of "As-Needed."

For each Scheduled process, describe the recurring due dates such as "the first Wednesday of every month." Defining the schedule will allow a parent process (how to send invoices) to create recurring child tasks (send invoices for January, send invoices for February).

How to add more attributes to your processes

Adding additional attributes during this step helps you analyze and improve your processes in the future. For example, you could tag processes that use batches with the "batch: yes" attribute. Then if you want to reduce the production batch size, you can scan your Process Library and find all the relevant processes.

Only add attributes that are relevant to your business right now. You can start with just a few attributes and add more later.

How you store these attributes will depend on the software you use to build your Process Library. For example, you could use a "Priority" field with High, Medium, and Low options or use a "Labels" field that allows #high, #medium, or #low.

Process management software may offer more ways to manage process labels. For example, you could label all your payroll-related processes with #payroll or @payroll or finance: payroll. Then you can create a filter to view just the processes with that label.

Resource attributes

Processes can share resources such as software applications, machines, supplies, forms, spreadsheets, websites, and documents.

You can label all the processes that use a shared resource, such as your accounting software or a piece of equipment. Then when you need to train someone on how to use that resource, you have quick access to all the related processes. If you need to replace or update a resource, you know all the processes that will be affected.

Functional area attributes

Every process that your business runs should fall into one and only one functional area. For example, "How to pay invoices" would be categorized under Finance. If you have several related processes within one functional area, you may wish to add a subarea such as Accounts Payable.

But what about processes that span multiple functional areas? For example, these processes involve multiple areas:

- "How to onboard a new employee" includes process steps related to finance, training, information technology, and client services.
- "How to fulfill a customer order" involves sales, production, and finance.
- "How to update the strategic plan" spans marketing, sales, finance, and client services.

- "How to develop a new product" requires input from marketing, engineering, purchasing, and manufacturing.

Each process will have a unique Process ID and a "home base" in one functional area. In a school library, a reference book is shelved in just one place. But many students can use the book for multiple research assignments.

Likewise, assigning a process to one functional area does not limit that process to being used only in one way or by just one role. For each process, pick the most sensible functional area based on where the process begins, where the process ends, or the location of related processes. For the example processes above,

- "How to onboard a new employee" could be under Human Resources or Administration.
- "How to fulfill a customer order" could be under Sales, Customer Fulfillment, Client Services, Manufacturing, or Production.
- "How to update the strategic plan" could be under Governance, Management, Administration, or Finance.
- "How to develop a new product" could be under Research & Development, Marketing, or Manufacturing.

You could also choose the functional area based on where the person assigned to the process works most of the time.

Focus area attributes

The Process Matrix introduced the four passive levels of focus for a process: Strategy, Planning, Analysis, or Operations. You can add one of these focus attributes for each process. For example, the process for "How to find and develop a new product" belongs to the Strategy focus area since launching a new product has long-term implications.

This gives you another way to search and filter your processes. If you're evaluating new analytics software, you can ask, "What are all our Analysis processes?" If you're setting the agenda for a strategy session, ask, "What are all our Strategy processes?"

Subarea attributes

The four levels of focus (Strategy, Planning, Analysis, and Operations) provide a way to categorize your processes within one functional area. However, you still may have dozens of processes within one functional area and focus level, such as Finance Operations. Create subareas to group similar processes within a functional area. If you find several related processes without a subarea, create a new subarea for those processes.

Store the subarea for each process as an attribute in your Process Library.

Cost attributes

Labeling the approximate cost of a process, even in terms of High, Medium, or Low, can help when you begin to prioritize your processes for improvement. Cost attributes include the following:

- Setup: How much does it cost to get this process ready to run?
- Per cycle: How much does it cost to run this process once?
- Per period: What is the cost per unit time (e.g., day, week, month, year) to run this process?
- Switching: How much does it cost to stop working on this process and start working on another one?

Role and people attributes

These attributes help you understand who is involved with running a process. After identifying the primary assignee role for a process, you can add more details about who else is involved.

- Assignee role. Who typically runs this process?
- Owner role. Who is responsible for directing, monitoring, and improving this process? The owner can be different than the assignee.
- Other roles. What other roles are involved with this process, including secondary or backup roles?
- Number of roles involved. How many roles are affected by this process?

- Number of people involved. How many people are affected by this process?
- Internal vs. External. Is this process completed in-house, or is it outsourced?

Time attributes

There are several time-related attributes that may be helpful to capture.

- Frequency: How often is this process run?
- Schedule: Is this process scheduled? If so, what is the schedule?
- Startup: How much time does it take to begin working on this process?
- Changeover: How much time does it take to switch from this process to another?
- Duration per client: How long does this process take per client?
- Duration per cycle: How long does this process take per occurrence?
- Service Level Agreements: Are there contractual commitments related to response time, delivery time, or uptime?
- Work session duration: How long does someone work on this process before needing a break?

Documentation attributes

These attributes can identify which How-to Guides need attention or corrective action.

- Completeness: How much more documentation does this process need?
- Update: Is an update needed?
- Diagram: Is a diagram or illustration needed?
- Suggestion: What could make this process better?
- Idea: What new or improved method could apply to this process?

Workflow attributes

These attributes describe how a process progresses from start to finish. You can use these attributes to find and eliminate bottlenecks shared by multiple processes.

- Initiator: How do we determine when to run this process? Who requests this process?
- Destination: Where do the outputs of this process go? Who receives the results of this process?
- Variability: How many combinations or variations of this process exist? When is each variation used?
- Approvals: Does the input, work-in-progress, or output need approval?
- People dependencies: What other people are needed to run this process?
- Process dependencies: What other processes does this process depend on?

Method attributes

These attributes identify techniques and approaches (both good and bad) that are used to run a process.

- Batch work: Is this process completed in batches? If so, what is the batch size?
- Batch method: How do you determine the size and composition of each batch?
- Controls and checks: Is there a standard quality check performed on this process?
- Automation: Is this process automated or partly automated? What automation tools are used?

Score attributes

You may want to flag processes based on criticality, complexity, or scalability. You can tag a process as Yes-No or High-Medium-Low for these attributes. But if you need finer-grained analysis, create a 1 to 4 (or 1 to 10) score for any attribute.

You can also create a score by combining several attributes. For example, you can create a process complexity score based on the number of people involved and the process duration. You can create a score for automation potential based on processes with high "time to complete" and high "ease of automation."

Priority attributes

Based on the above attributes, you can decide which processes need immediate attention and which are okay for now. If you see a process that needs an urgent fix, make a note by adding an "urgent" label. Then filter your processes by that label to create a prioritized action plan.

How to benefit from your process attributes

All these useful descriptors of your processes are not meant to be displayed behind glass in your Process Museum. You can use your process attributes as a key part of running and improving your business. You can sort, filter, and search your Process Library to evaluate your process effectiveness and answer these vital questions:

- Assignments. Do we know who's doing what, and when?
- Priority. What should we improve first?
- Organization. Are we capturing our process knowledge?

You can look at all your processes and get a holistic view of how your business runs. See your business as a collection of integrated processes that produce results. So far, we have used the following hierarchy shown in Figure 8-2 to identify your processes:

Figure 8-2. Process Identification Hierarchy. Gather useful process attributes to further develop your organization's process hierarchy.

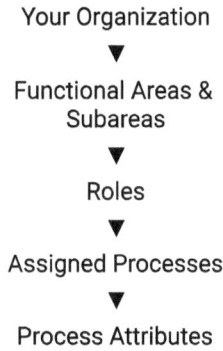

Your Organization
▼
Functional Areas &
Subareas
▼
Roles
▼
Assigned Processes
▼
Process Attributes

Now that you have a Process Library with a variety of process attributes, you can think strategically about your processes from different perspectives. Figure 8-3 shows six ways to view your processes.

Figure 8-3. Six Ways to View Processes. View your processes in several different ways after adding attributes.

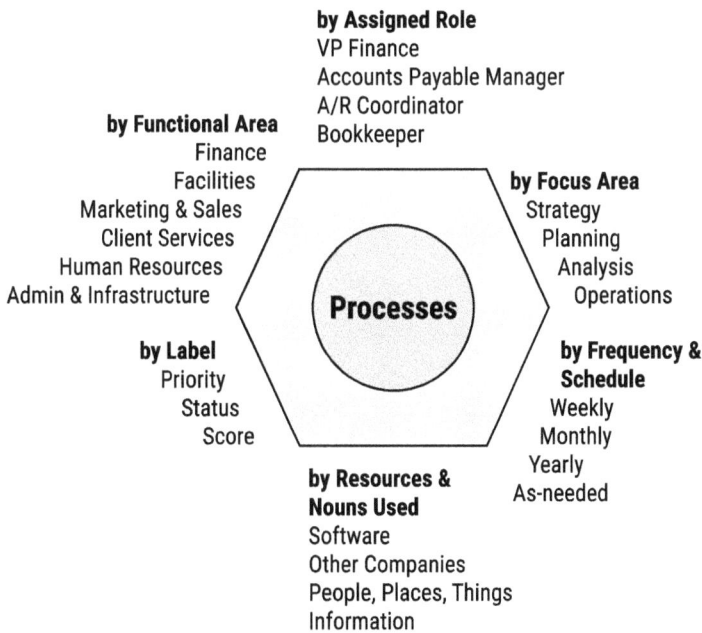

by Assigned Role
VP Finance
Accounts Payable Manager
A/R Coordinator
Bookkeeper

by Functional Area
Finance
Facilities
Marketing & Sales
Client Services
Human Resources
Admin & Infrastructure

by Focus Area
Strategy
Planning
Analysis
Operations

Processes

by Label
Priority
Status
Score

**by Frequency &
Schedule**
Weekly
Monthly
Yearly
As-needed

**by Resources &
Nouns Used**
Software
Other Companies
People, Places, Things
Information

These views can help you generate new ideas for improving results, reducing risk, and growing faster.

Checklist for describing your processes with attributes

☐ Create a short ID for every process

☐ Add a frequency for every recurring process

☐ Add at least one label for each process

☐ Add subareas as needed

☐ Add process attributes to your Process Library

Chapter 9

How to Describe Your Processes Using How-To Guides

Identify	Describe	Use	Improve
Chapter 4. Identify Your **Functional Areas**	Chapter 8. Describe Your Processes With **Attributes**	Chapter 10. Use Your Processes in **Day-to-Day Work**	Chapter 13. **Improve** Your Processes
Chapter 5. Identify Your **Roles**		Chapter 11. Use Your Processes With **Your Team**	Chapter 14. Improve Your Processes by **Learning from Others**
Chapter 6. Identify Your **Processes**	Chapter 9. Describe Your Processes Using **How-To Guides**		
Chapter 7. Identify **Gaps and Opportunities**		Chapter 12. Use Your Processes With **Business Frameworks**	Chapter 15. Improve Your Processes Using **External Resources**

This chapter describes how to create a How-to Guide for each process. A How-to Guide can start as a simple document and become more detailed over time.

I met with a client to understand and capture his process for "How to create a project proposal." He told me, "I don't need a How-to Guide for this. I've done this hundreds of times. I already know how!"

But he was the only one who knew how to create a proposal. What if he wasn't available or wanted someone else to help? When we began exploring his step-by-step sequence for creating a new project proposal, we discovered that many of the finer points were solely in his brain, invisible to the rest of the world. Here are some of the things he knew how to do but were not written down.

- How to find the proposal templates in a shared folder
- How to pick the right template to use based on the type of project
- How to modify the template based on the client's needs
- How to rename and store the customized proposal
- How to sign and send the proposal to the client
- How to receive and log the accepted proposal
- How to share the signed proposal with the client
- How to kick off the project

We also discovered that he didn't perform these steps the same way every time. This inconsistency slowed things down. As we quickly wrote down the steps listed above, a How-to Guide emerged. Now he can refine his process to complete project proposals faster and with more consistency.

This story illustrates the importance of describing each process. You need to capture process steps with enough detail so that someone else can follow your instructions to run the process. We've laid the foundation by identifying processes and adding some attributes. Now it's time to add the nitty-gritty of how these processes work.

Document while innovating

You may think, "I can't document and standardize things while I'm still innovating. I can't describe the thing and build the thing at the same time!"

Operating and innovating at the same time requires a "paradox mindset."[1] Toyota manages to achieve the dual goals of maintaining stability while also encouraging constant reform. As former chairperson, Hiroshi Okuda put it, "Reform business when business is good."

I publish a monthly report for one of my businesses. If I were starting with zero documentation for how to run that process, it would be hard to write down instructions for that report while I'm actually doing the work. That might slow me down so much that I'd miss the publication deadline.

But when I started this process from scratch, I first captured the basic flow of how I created the report, section by section. This was only a few lines of notes per section. I also referred to my notes from when I designed the report. This allowed me to create an outline with only high-level tasks and not all the details.

When I ran the process the next month, I added a few sub-items and more details. I focused on the most difficult and error-prone sections. After several months of running that report, I had a detailed How-to Guide. I continue to refer to that guide and make tweaks each month.

Preserve the 'art' and document the 'science'

If your business relies on creativity to provide customized solutions to clients, you may think, "My business is more art than science."

Your workflow may look like this:

1. Your customer comes to you with a need.
2. You do the magic that only you can do.
3. You share the amazing result with your customer.

The "magic" is the artistry that requires your skill or supernatural ability. It may be difficult or impossible to write down how the magic works, but even the most artistic, quirky business needs processes.

My friend Eric is a metal sculptor. He starts with a concept and then creates a sculpture from steel or bronze. These are often large pieces that require a crane to move. It seems he's limited only by his imagination because his creative process is organic, free-form, and intangible. But his creativity is not completely unbounded. He makes several decisions before he begins work on a sculpture. These decisions are more science than art. What material will I be using? What size sculpture will this be? What has the client requested?

To fulfill a sculpture commission, he must follow a set of steps.

- Interview the client to clarify expectations
- Decide project constraints. These include total cost, target price, size, materials, time available, and client preferences
- Order materials and supplies
- Schedule design time and get ready to create
- *The Artistic Magic Happens Here*
- Fabricate the sculpture
- Perform finishing tasks such as painting
- Prepare the sculpture for shipment
- Deliver and install the sculpture
- Invoice the customer

Many creative activities happen during the "Magic Happens Here" step. But other things happen before and after that step. How can these other process steps be simplified? By making the things outside of the "magic" step easier, the artist gains more time and freedom to make the magic that the customers pay for.

An artist's magic could be a sculpture, song, or painting. It is the other steps in the process that affect how many customers can enjoy the magic and how profitable the magic is for the artist.

How to get started with process documentation

One complaint about documentation is that it's too difficult to create. Converting thoughts and ideas into written words is a struggle for some people. Someone may be brilliant when working with people, equipment, or software, but they may lack the skills to describe their knowledge in writing. Let's explore some ideas to make capturing your organization's expertise easier.

Keep it simple to start

Initially, just add basic instructions for each process.

- How do you start the process?
- What do you do after that?
- How do you finish the process?

Focus on the key steps. You can fill in more detail later. The aphorism "well begun is half done" comes to mind. Once I start writing something, I can more easily think about what to add or how to improve what I wrote.

Don't aim for perfection

The prospect of writing down "everything" for a process gives me heartburn or maybe even an ulcer. But is the only alternative writing down *nothing*? No. This is a false dichotomy.

Unless you're writing the manual for a jet engine or a heart-lung machine, start with something basic and incomplete. Then improve it over time. Something is better than nothing. Capture the essence of how to complete the process. If you had two minutes to give an overview of how a process works, what would you say? Capture that information.

Don't be afraid to start with something that's rubbish. Don't overthink it. Just write down something helpful. At least you'll have some material to work with instead of a blank page.

The Italian proverb "Le meglio è l'inimico del bene" is translated as "the best is the enemy of the good." In other words, start with something (anything!) and then work to improve it.[2]

Let's explore how you could start with *something*.

- Can you ask the creator of the process how they would run it?
- If the process involves technology or equipment, did the manufacturer give you any instructions?
- If an outside company runs the process, what is the best way to work with them?
- Can you write down the main steps?

Use alternative capture methods and media

The Process Prescription requires you to capture information. But if your team members are reluctant to write things down, how can you capture your process details?

Justin is an example of someone who doesn't like to write. He has atrocious spelling and poor grammar skills and would not know where to begin to document a process. However, he's a senior manager at a commercial services company. He has a natural talent for understanding customer needs, troubleshooting problems, mentoring team members, and motivating people. In other words, he gets the job done and is a valuable contributor to the company.

But if he can't (or won't) write down his processes, how can you capture the things Justin does so well and so quickly? Since he dislikes writing, consider other ways to capture his process knowledge.

- Use video
  - Shoot a quick video of him describing the process. If you keep this short and to the point, this does not need editing.
  - Use screen recording software to create a video showing how to use an application or a website.
- Use audio
  - Record a voice memo and have someone else transcribe it.
  - Add voice notations to photos.
  - Use the speech-to-text (voice dictation) feature in a word processor or mobile notes app.
- Use images and photos
  - Snap a photo that shows what to do, or take before-and-after photos.
  - Grab a screenshot. To explain how to do something online, capture the whole window or just a portion of the page.
  - Jot down the main points on the back of a receipt and take a photo.
  - Use a notebook or notepad. List the basic process steps as they occur. Take a photo of the notes.

- ○   Create a drawing or flowchart to explain how to run a process. Take a photo of your drawing and paste it into a How-to Guide. Add descriptions and captions. Re-draw sketches as digital graphics if you want to continue to improve the drawing.
- Use an app
  - ○   Use a note-taking app to capture the key process steps.

Capture the variation

Does your work seem random sometimes? Is the randomness unavoidable?

You may think, "There's too much variation in what we do to have a standard process."

Let's consider jobs with a wide variety of tasks and a broad mix of activities. What's the most "random" type of job?

- Could it be a handyman who works on many different home repairs?
- Could it be the concierge at a luxury hotel who gets all sorts of weird requests from high-maintenance guests?
- Could it be the emergency room doctor who sees dozens of different cases on a single shift?
- Or could it be the small business consultant who advises many types of businesses?

To a degree, all these jobs must deal with anything that comes through the door.

But there are not an *infinite* number of possibilities. While no two customers or clients are identical, there are patterns.

The handyman's tasks fall into categories based on the systems in a house, such as plumbing, electrical, and carpentry.

The concierge's tasks all involve helping the guests do something or get something: tickets, reservations, directions, gifts, or food. The concierge can pre-plan the best and fastest way to resolve these scenarios.

The doctor's diagnoses each have a diagnosis-related group (DRG) code, and each code has a specified price that appears on the patient's bill.

The small business consultant sees similar marketing problems across his entire client base.

I'm not suggesting that these jobs are simple and formulaic. There's a lot of variation. But there are patterns to find and optimize. Capture the variations, then look for patterns and common threads. Find ways to standardize while still producing the different outputs that your customers need.

Don't worry about grammar and formatting

If your grammar or spelling is terrible, don't sweat it. Use the built-in grammar tool in your editing software. Also, don't judge others who don't write as well as you do. Be gracious. We all have unique abilities and talents.

Some people can format a list of simple instructions without being too wordy. For others, it's a struggle to begin.

The celebrated actress Helen Hayes said, "The expert at anything was once a beginner."[3] The more you practice, the better you get. Keep plugging away at your How-to Guides. Practice makes progress.

Team up to help each other

Software developers sometimes use a technique called "pair programming" to benefit from the abilities of two people simultaneously. Here are some ideas for how to pair up with someone to describe your processes:

- Explain the process to someone else and have them write it down. This person could be someone less experienced who is learning the process or someone you're teaching how to run the process. This person could be your assistant, colleague, new hire, or someone you want to cross-train as a backup. This collaboration is a good test to see if you can explain your process steps in an understandable way. If this person has skills that you lack, they can add helpful details. The two of you can make a lot of progress together.
- Interview someone else who also knows how to run your process and write down what they say. Compare how they describe the

process with how you run the process. What do you do that is similar? What would you do differently?

- Have someone interview you to identify the steps in your processes.
- Have someone follow you around for a day. This "understudy" could be an intern, a new hire, someone who reports to you, or a consultant. Teach your follower how things work. Have your follower take notes and ask questions. Verify that they understand how each process runs and that their notes capture what they learn.
- Interview your boss. Ask, "What do you think I do?" That will provide an overview of the inputs and outputs of your position. Use that as a starting point for adding more details about your processes.

Make quick lists

To create a How-to Guide, make lists that describe the process. For example,

- What's the list of things you must do before you run this process?
- What's the list of materials or inputs you need before running this process?
- What's the list of training or preparation steps that someone must complete before running this process?
- What's the list of steps to complete this process?
- What's the list of errors that can occur during this process?
- What's the list of things you should check after you run this process?
- Who should you contact if you need help running this process?

When starting your process documentation, you don't need to number the items on your list. Instead, make lists with bullets or checkboxes. You can make a quick checklist by using two underscores to start each item, like this:

```
__ First, do this
__ Then do this
```

Even if you're reading the checklist items on a screen and you don't tick off the items with a pen, the underscores serve as a reminder that these are action steps you need to complete.

Use paper when it makes sense

For some processes, paper instructions and checklists are more accessible, transportable, and editable. With paper, you can make a quick handwritten note or diagram while you're working. After you've run the process a few times, update the digital version based on your edits.

Another benefit of paper is that the cost of a printed page is a tiny fraction of a screen. With paper you don't have to worry about breakage or needing electricity.

Paper allows you to put the instructions where the work gets done. For example, you could document the "how to clean the kitchen" process by creating a one-page How-to Guide with photos of the process steps. Laminate and post that page on the fridge.

Include the process ID on anything you print so that you can find the original if you need to make edits or print another copy.

Hire a documentation consultant

If you find it tough to get started, a documentation specialist can help you get organized and gain momentum. But don't rely on them as a crutch. While a consultant can get you started and provide you with the best practices for your industry, it's up to your team to maintain your Process Library and How-to Guides. Don't completely outsource your process documentation, especially for those processes that are core to your business. Instead, develop a culture that values continuous improvement, learning, and documentation. Without a commitment from inside your organization, your written processes will collect dust.

How to create a How-to Guide using a template

Once you have completed a few process interviews, you can create a fill-in-the-blank template to standardize how you capture process documentation.

Here are sections you can include in a How-to Guide template.

- Process ID and process name
- Purpose. Why do we do this? Who does this help or benefit?
- Schedule. When do we do this? Is this done as-needed or on a schedule?
- Getting started. What do I need to work on this? What tools, equipment, software, websites, documents, or other how-to guides do I need?
- Process steps. What are the steps to complete this? What is the sequence from start to finish? This can include images and diagrams.
- Alerts
    ◦ Should an important step be flagged for special attention?
    ◦ Should a step be marked as essential, recommended, or optional?
    ◦ What precautions should be taken?
    ◦ Should a step be marked as difficult, dangerous, or error-prone?
- Success Criteria
    ◦ What is the desired outcome?
    ◦ How should I evaluate the outcome? Do I inspect, measure, review, or use a checklist?
- Troubleshooting
    ◦ What should I do if I encounter a problem?
    ◦ What types of problems, errors, exceptions, or variations can I expect?
    ◦ When a problem occurs, what should I document? (e.g., date, description, cause, fix)

- Support Resources. What resources can I use? (e.g., websites, books, manuals, guides, online forums)
- Internal Support. Who do I contact if I need help? In what situations should I contact them? (e.g., missing part, broken equipment, error, anomaly)
- External Support. Who can I contact outside the company? (e.g., technical support, vendor rep, consultant)

The length of a How-to Guide depends on what's being documented. Some of my How-to Guides are less than one page, and one is over 50 pages long. Figure 9-1 shows a page from a sample How-to Guide.

Figure 9-1. Sample How-to Guide. Use a template with headings and sections, then fill in the details.

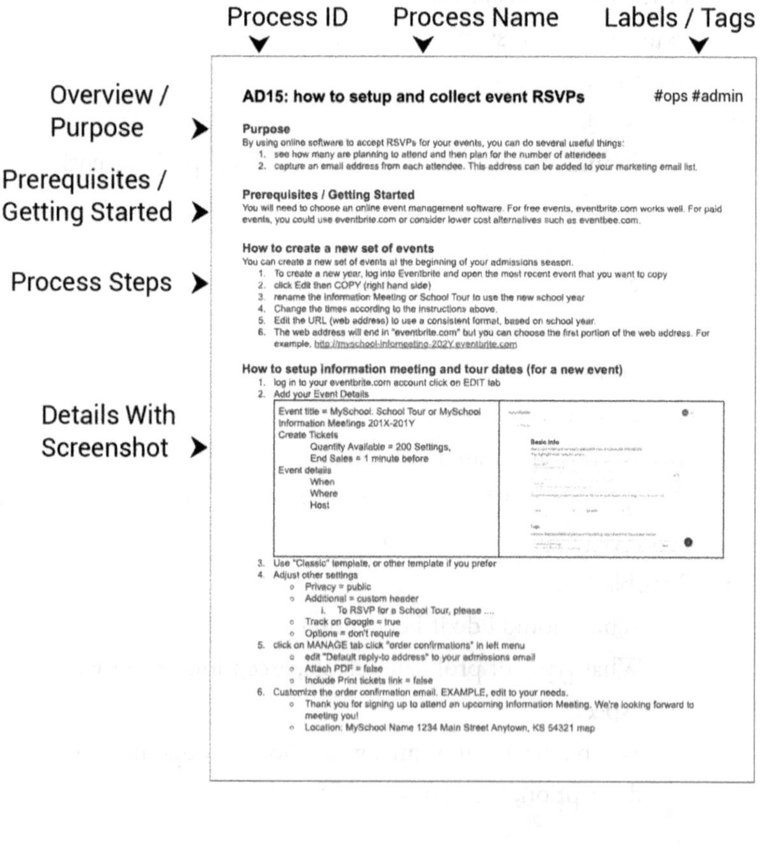

How to create shared folders for your How-to Guides

You may ask, "Where do we put all these How-to Guides we're creating?"

There are specialized software solutions for knowledge management, but these are not needed to get started. You can use your existing document management software to store your How-to Guides. Create a folder for each functional area in your existing document repository. For example, an organization with five functional areas could setup these shared folders:

▸ PF: Production & Fulfillment
▸ MS: Marketing & Sales
▸ IN: Infrastructure
▸ FI: Finance
▸ MG: Management

Because the five functional areas don't overlap, every shared file in your entire organization can be placed into one of these folders.

Within each area folder, create one subfolder to hold the How-to Guides (the "verbs") for that area. Then create a "noun" subfolder for each type of thing or dataset that you deal with in that area. For example, the folders in the Finance area might look like this:

▾ FI: Finance
    ▸ _FI How-to Guides
    ▸ Accounting
    ▸ Insurance
    ▸ Reporting
    ▸ Subscriptions
    ▸ Taxes
    ▸ Vendors

This approach organizes your How-to Guides in a separate folder under each area. Each noun has its own folder to group similar items together. Under each noun folder, you can create a folder for each year if you want to archive old documents and reduce clutter.

Organize your existing files by placing them into the proper folder. Associate existing documents with their corresponding process by adding the process ID to the document name or description.

You'll also need to apply the correct permissions to the folders and files so that everyone can access what they need while protecting sensitive information. If you have several groups of people that need varying access to different folders, create a permissions matrix that shows who gets access to what folders. Sync that matrix with the folder permissions in your document management system. You can also ask your IT person to do this.

Create a process for how you will organize your process documentation. Include the following:

- How to name folders
- How to organize the folder hierarchy
- How to set up folder-sharing policies by role
- How to backup folders and files
- How to archive old documents

How to write better How-to Guides

Include transitions between steps

Specify what someone needs to do to finish a process step and move to the next step. Explain how to close down, clean up, or put away the items from the previous step. For example, an online process to file taxes might include "click [Continue] at the bottom of the screen." What seems obvious to you might not be obvious to the next person, so lean toward being precise without being wordy.

Don't Repeat Yourself (D.R.Y.)

Efficient computer programmers don't repeat the same lines of code over and over in their programs. Instead, they put pieces of reusable content in modules, classes, objects, templates, and libraries. In the same way, you can re-use instructions in your How-to Guides. Identify reusable sections using bookmarks, labels, tags, or even separate documents. The exact method will depend on your document management system. Then link to that section when you need it, without repeating it. When the instructions in that section need updating, you only have to make changes in one place.

An example of DRY is a private school that uses email templates. They use standard messages to accept prospective students, send payment reminders, and make announcements. They can store all their standard messages in a template repository to use when running their recurring communications processes.

Use screenshots

A screenshot can show how to interact with software, such as how to fill out a form. But don't overdo it with these. A screenshot can be overkill if you're providing simple instructions. For example, if you're describing how to submit a form, you could simply write in the How-to Guide: "At the bottom of the page, click the blue [Submit] button." You don't need a screenshot to explain that.

Use video

I usually prefer a written list of instructions since that's a compact format for quick reference. But in some cases, a visual is better. If a picture is worth a thousand words, is a video worth ten thousand? A video can work well when showing something for the first time or describing how to work with a physical object. But don't complicate things. Please don't make me watch a 5-minute video to learn how to fill out a 1-minute form. Instead, could you put instructions on the form itself? Or add pop-up instructions for each online form field? Or link to instructions for each field? Or create a reference guide for the form? Or create a checklist?

You can combine media for the best results. For example, use a video for an introduction and initial training, but then supplement it with a written How-to Guide, Quick Reference Guide, and checklist.

Checklist for describing your processes using How-to Guides

- ☐ Use a How-to Guide template when creating new How-to Guides.
- ☐ Overrule the template as needed. Use the parts that are most valuable and delete irrelevant sections.
- ☐ Start small. Don't get bogged down trying to create a perfect document.
- ☐ Organize your shared files in folders that match your functional areas.
- ☐ Use multiple types of media to describe your processes, as needed.

Chapter 10

How to Use Your Processes in Day-to-Day Work

Identify	Describe	Use	Improve
Chapter 4. Identify Your **Functional Areas**		Chapter 10. Use Your Processes in **Day-to-Day Work**	Chapter 13. **Improve** Your Processes
Chapter 5. Identify Your **Roles**	Chapter 8. Describe Your Processes With **Attributes**	Chapter 11. Use Your Processes With **Your Team**	Chapter 14. Improve Your Processes by **Learning from Others**
Chapter 6. Identify Your **Processes**	Chapter 9. Describe Your Processes Using **How-To Guides**	Chapter 12. Use Your Processes With **Business Frameworks**	Chapter 15. Improve Your Processes Using **External Resources**
Chapter 7. Identify **Gaps and Opportunities**			

The Process Prescription applies to day-to-day work at every level of your organization. Both executive and front-line workers can benefit from having a process mindset.

As you begin to apply the Process Prescription across your organization, encourage people at every level to create and use How-to Guides. Build a culture of process thinking where it's normal for everyone to find ways to simplify and improve.

In this chapter, you'll learn how to use your processes by including How-to Guides as part of your daily work.

How to use How-to Guides while you work

With the Identify and Describe steps complete, your team members should begin to use the How-to Guides as part of their daily work.

As you run a process, follow the steps in the corresponding How-to Guide. If you discover a missing, unclear, or inaccurate step, fix it while you work. If you don't have time, mark it for editing later. Always make a note if something is not quite right. Don't leave it for the next person to figure out.

Have the How-to Guide open while completing a process. Dan Martell, an entrepreneur and small business expert, uses this approach:

"If a procedure exists for the work you're about to do, you must have it open. It has to be sitting there, and you have to reference it so you can actually ensure that each step of the work gets done. And if there's an issue where you say 'go to this screen' and the screen has changed in the software, you can update it in real-time."[1]

Your access to How-to Guides can vary based on whether you work at a desk, in a factory, in a vehicle, on the sales floor, or a job site. Experiment to find the best method for accessing your How-to Guides. You may choose to use a combination of software, screens, and paper. Your goal is to get quick access to the right How-to Guide at the right time.

Even if you have memorized all the steps of a process, continue using a completion checklist so you're not under the pressure of needing to remember every step every time. Each checklist item can link to a detailed description if you need it.

To test a How-to Guide, have someone other than the primary assignee follow the process. This should uncover anything that is missing or unclear. By having multiple people use and improve the same How-to Guide, you get several benefits:

- More accurate and understandable How-to Guides that are easy to use.
- More useful How-to Guides for training, cross-skilling, and job sharing.
- More ideas for improvement.
- More interesting work. You get more variety, more knowledge, more opportunities to collaborate, more challenges, and more ways to provide input and ideas.

How to update your How-to Guides

As you use your How-to Guides, continue to review them with a critical eye toward refinement. You can set goals for improving your team's How-to Guides. For example, each team member can choose one process per month to review in-depth. If you have ten people in your group, that's 120 process reviews per year. To support this effort, create a How-to Guide for "How to review and update a process." Below is a version of how that might look.

MG17: how to review and update a process

1. Choose a process to review based on priority. Choose at least one process per month.
2. Open the How-to Guide and follow the steps in the process. If it's not the right time to actually complete each step, then visualize yourself working through the process steps.
3. Answer the following questions about the process:
    ◦ Are any steps unclear?
    ◦ Are any steps missing?
    ◦ Are any steps inaccurate?

- ○ Are all the process attributes accurate? (e.g., frequency, assignee, labels)
- ○ Is the completion checklist accurate?
4. Add the date and your name at the top of the How-to Guide (or in your process management system) to indicate you have reviewed the process.

If your organization requires approval to change process documentation, add a note requesting the change.

How to add helpful details

As you use a process, see if there's anything you can add or edit to make things easier. Here are some ways I like to improve How-to Guides:

- Add tips for quick setup. What should be done before I begin the process to make the work easier? For example, what browser tabs do I need open? How should I arrange the tools I need?
- Keep headings updated. If a section heading or page title no longer matches the underlying content, change it.
- Put "where" before "how." Before I can work on something, I need to be in the right place. First, explain where to run the process, then list what to do. If the instructions are for using software, explain how to get to the proper screen or tab.
- Consider the options. If there are multiple ways to complete a process, I make sure to capture the variations so I can figure out which method is best and delete the others. I can also describe when to apply different scenarios.
- Re-order the process steps. Sometimes I can rearrange the process steps into a more logical order that allows me to work faster. I can make a note of ways to work ahead while I'm waiting for something else to finish.

How to flag variances and frustrations

Never ignore a poor or frustrating process. At the very least, make a note. When you ignore out-of-date references, broken links, and unclear sections in a How-to Guide, you create problems in the future. Over time, the How-to Guide becomes inaccurate and less useful. Use labels or comments (such as #update, #fix, or #clarify) to tag a problem. Also, add your thoughts about a possible solution. Even if you don't have time to fix the problem then and there, don't miss the chance to capture your valuable insights.

How to create troubleshooting guides

You can create a section in each How-to Guide for what to do if the unexpected happens. When something unusual happens, write down the date and how you handled the situation. This creates a log of known problems and the corresponding solution. Refer to this collection of solutions when trying to fix similar things in the future. Over time, you can look for patterns to find common solutions.

Software engineers use the term "edge case" to refer to scenarios where things break or behave weirdly if the input is too high, too low, or unexpected. Such a case contrasts with the typical, everyday situation where everything works fine. If you can only succeed with perfect weather, blue skies, and a cool breeze, then your business is too fragile. As author Nicolas Taleb puts it, we need to be "anti-fragile." Our processes need to be resilient and self-correcting.

A simple format for adding a troubleshooting section to a How-to Guide is this:
- If you see unusual thing A, then do B.
- If you see unusual thing C, then do D.

Repeat this pattern as many times as needed for all the scenarios you encounter.

When I worked at McDonald's, we occasionally saw tour buses pull into the parking lot. This is an edge case: dozens of hungry people would soon be standing four-deep in front of the cash registers and ordering lots of food within minutes of each other.

Our manager knew what to do when she saw this. She called back to the kitchen: "I need a twelve turn-lay on the 10-to-1 grill." This was an order for 12 hamburgers and 12 more after the first batch had been flipped on the grill. This was usually followed by directions to make a large batch of fries and McNuggets. She gave the kitchen a head start before the food orders started rolling in. Her experience allowed her to have a consistent response to an edge case, namely, "if you see a tour bus in your parking lot, then start grilling 24 hamburgers." With busloads of people, it was a safe bet that we would use all those beef patties to make hamburgers, cheeseburgers, and Big Macs.

Create a sequence of "things to try" when troubleshooting a piece of equipment. Write down what you do, what works, and what doesn't. For example, here's a simplified version of what I do when my home printer stops working:

1. Make sure the printer is turned on and connected to the home network. Also, check and resolve any error messages on the printer's display panel.

2. Get the printer's Internet protocol (IP) address using the printer's control panel.

3. Ping the printer from your computer. If you can't, resolve the network connection and try again. If you can ping the printer but still can't print, then...

4. Delete and re-add the printer from Settings. If you still can't print, then...

5. Check the security settings. If you still can't print, then...

6. Switch the software interface used to talk to the printer.

I can quickly get my printer back online by following this "how to troubleshoot the printer" guide. It was a frustrating, hit-or-miss mess when I first wrote it down. As I have added improvements, new steps, and additional details over the years, I know I can calmly get my printer back online in just a few minutes.

Another example involves a monthly report that I generate. Making the report involves several different number-crunching programs and dozens of steps. I usually encounter some type of error every few months. Each time,

I log the error and the date it occurs. I've collected a thorough list of possible problems, such as the following:

- If you get the error "Error: package or namespace load failed"...
- If you get the error "ModuleNotFoundError"...
- If you get the error "Error in scan"
- If you cannot run the script...
- If you see an incorrect date...

Since those errors are already quite boring, I won't subject you to the equally boring descriptions of how I solved them. But writing down how to I fixed each error saved me several hours in a few cases when I encountered the same error, even years later.

How to link your processes to resources

You can link useful resources to each process for quick access. By resource, I mean anything that helps run the process. Resources include information (software, websites, spreadsheets, files, databases, documents), things (tools, supplies, equipment), and people (contractors, experts, colleagues, consultants).

Add links in the How-to Guide to online resources. Link to resource documents instead of making a copy. This prevents you from wasting time maintaining two copies of the same information.

Provide explicit instructions about how to access each resource. Include what to do if the resource is unavailable or misplaced.

How to use complementary software

The Process Prescription works alongside your existing systems and other software tools. Here's how you can use the Process Prescription to leverage three types of software.

Operational software

This is software that runs one or more of your functional areas. You may have specialized software unique to your industry that manages your core information. For example, hospitals have Electronic Health Record systems, and banks have Core Banking systems.

Maximize the benefits of your core applications by using the Process Prescription to do the following:

- Capture the knowledge or "Brainware" required to run your software and produce useful results
- Define processes for feeding the software what it needs
- Define processes for using the software's output
- Document how your different software packages talk to each other
- Capture how to troubleshoot errors, bugs, outages, and weird output

Process management software

This software focuses on organizing, describing, and improving your processes. This type of software helps you build and maintain your Process Library. We'll look at process management software in more depth in Chapter 15.

Use process management software to organize your Process Library, choose process improvement opportunities, and track your progress. Before you start adding new software tools, establish clear objectives and plans. Even if the software you plan to use is low-cost or open-source, you don't want to waste your time pursuing low-value improvements.

The psychologist Abraham Maslow wrote, "I suppose it is tempting if the only tool you have is a hammer, to treat everything as if it were a nail."[2] It's tempting to apply a new software tool to anything in sight. Identify your processes and understand your needs before you spend time and money on new software. Otherwise, you risk being pulled in the direction of the person who's screaming the loudest or the software vendor who's applying the most pressure.

Productivity software

You can use your office software and productivity tools to implement the Process Prescription. Take care to avoid two pitfalls: 1) creating unshared islands of information and 2) sharing messages and files without linking to their related processes.

Consider using the following techniques as you manage documents, messages, and tasks in a process-centric way:

- Create shared folders that correspond to your functional areas.
- Store How-to Guides and related files in shared folders. Don't let hundreds of files float around in personal folders.
- Use your Process Library to link files and resources to their corresponding processes.
- Use messaging (email, chat, video, voice) primarily for notifications and reminders.
- Don't use email for discussions and sharing notes. Instead, preserve discussions and notes in a format that can be shared and linked directly to the related processes.
- Don't use email for making requests and sending approvals. Instead, use a workflow system that allows everyone to see the status of their current open items.
- Don't use email to provide detailed instructions. Instead, link to a shared How-to Guide.
- Standardize your toolset. Decide on the best tool to use for file sharing, collaboration, and task management. Choose the best way to input data, create reports, update documents, and send notifications. Minimize cost and clutter by getting rid of duplicate tools.

You can combine productivity software and process management software to build a system that handles your How-to Guides, role assignments, and recurring tasks.

How to apply your processes across all levels

Let's look at three different roles (Operations Team Member, Manager, and Executive) to see how each person might use processes in their daily work.

If I'm an Operations Team Member, here are ways I can use processes to work smarter:

- Follow How-to Guides to complete my tasks.

- Update task deadlines on my personal calendar based on due dates on a shared calendar.
- Create a schedule or task checklist for the upcoming week based on all my roles and processes. I can also look ahead to prepare for processes that take multiple days to complete.
- Review all the processes in my role descriptions to make sure that the processes match what I'm expected to do.
- Update How-to Guides to reflect the way things really work. I can add clarifications, corrections, and suggestions.
- Link existing documentation to its corresponding process.

If I'm a Manager, I need to help people do their jobs and be as productive as possible. I can use processes to do the following:

- Conduct a walk-through of a complicated or error-prone process. Validate the accuracy of the process and look for improvement opportunities.
- Document best practices for key processes.
- Tag processes that need documentation or attention.
- Cross-train team members so that two people know how to do the same job.
- Track task completion by team members.
- Solicit feedback from my team about what frustrates them and how process changes could alleviate those frustrations.
- Encourage collaboration by having multiple people in the same role share the same process documentation.
- Evaluate the effectiveness of process owners. I can change the owner of a process if someone else would be a better fit.
- Find opportunities to reuse or combine similar processes.
- Develop training and onboarding packets using a collection of How-to Guides.

If I'm an Executive (or business owner), I need to guide my organization toward strategic goals, cast a vision, and remove obstacles. I can use processes to do the following:

- Ask questions to refine existing processes.

- Tag processes to review with my team and leadership. I can choose improvement initiatives based on processes with similar characteristics.
- Define objectives and key results (OKRs) related to process improvement.
- Design new processes to accomplish strategic objectives.
- Identify constraints at the process level that are limiting growth and profitability.
- Identify missing processes needed to pursue the company's vision and strategic plans. I can evaluate our set of existing processes at each focus level (Strategy, Planning, Analysis, Operations) to look for gaps and opportunities.
- Expand our team's skills so that we can meet our objectives.

How to overcome common challenges

As I have surveyed and worked with various businesses, some themes have emerged. When asked, "What's the most difficult part about using written processes, and why?" the answers tend to fall into three categories:

- It's difficult to organize and share processes
- It's difficult to keep processes accurate
- It's difficult to use processes in a fast-paced environment

How to organize and share your processes

Without a way to organize your process documents, it's difficult to find and share them. Your Process Library should provide an easy way to add and retrieve documents. You should be able to search for any topic or keyword and find the right document quickly.

In the last chapter, we covered how to create shared folders for your How-to Guides. Create additional folders for processes that require additional materials and resources.

You can supplement this approach with a process management system that adds process labels, IDs, filters, searches, and assigned roles. For example, you can create a list of How-to Guide links for each role. Anyone stepping into that role has quick access to all the How-to Guides they need.

Provide quick access to How-to Guides by making your Process Library available wherever the work is getting done: on the shop floor, on the go, at a desk, or in the classroom. Provide access from mobile devices, desktop computers, or printed guides based on what works best.

The worst scenario is when someone hoards their How-to Guides and resources in their personal folders and refuses to share. In the next chapter, we'll look at ways to share and collaborate.

How to keep your processes accurate

Trying to follow a How-to Guide with outdated instructions is frustrating. Another annoyance is dealing with a How-to Guide that skips steps and does not have enough detail. How can we keep How-to Guides updated and accurate?

Here are some suggestions for keeping your process documentation up-to-date.

Share the editing. Allow anyone involved with a process to provide input on that process. If the process is delicate or dangerous, such as "How to overhaul a jet engine," you may need to add an approval step for changes. If the process is routine, such as "How to create the monthly financial report," then the person working on the process should be able to improve it on-the-fly. If you need to roll back to an older version, use your document archive or the "edit history" function in your editing software. Most editing tools keep a log of who's changed what.

Capture comments. If allowing someone to edit a How-to Guide directly is not practical, then allow anyone to add a tag or comment with a suggestion. Work with your team to get rid of the idea that if they find a defect, then "somebody can fix that later." Everyone should describe problems they find while running a process. If there's time pressure and a How-to Guide can't be edited while running the process, at least make a quick note about the problem. You'll have that information when you want to improve the process. If someone comments, "Yeah, that's messed up, but it's not my area," then they are wasting an opportunity to help the business improve.

Use check-out questions. After you run a process, ask the following questions:

- Was there a step missing in the How-to Guide?
- Was there a variation or exception that was not mentioned in the How-to Guide?
- Was there anything that broke the process?
- Was there any vagueness or anything that forced you to make a judgment call?
- Was there anything that could be done better?

Question the relevance. If you find yourself saying, "Parts of this process aren't useful," then that's great! You may have found a way to save time by getting rid of a step. If you're in a rush, add a tag such as #relevant? and go back later to evaluate that process step.

How to use processes in a fast-paced environment

For some activities, it's hard to do something and follow a written process simultaneously. Here are some concerns from people who find it challenging to follow written processes:

- "My job doesn't allow me to read a process while working. It's too hard to use a process while I'm doing my job."
- "It's hard to follow a process if I have to keep referring to it."
- "My schedule is very busy, and there's little time to look up a written procedure."
- "When you have to read instructions in front of a customer, it's more stressful and makes it look like you don't know how to do your job."
- "It's hard when you're on the spot and need to do something fast for a customer who is waiting in front of you."
- "The process takes a long time to read and memorize."
- "Following the process is too time-consuming. It's tedious and slow."

You need to follow your processes while you're working. But with some jobs, referring to a written guide while working is not practical.

When retail salespeople are helping customers find clothing to try on in a boutique, they are not referring to a "How to Sell" guide.

When alpine skiers barrel down a mountain while competing in the giant slalom, they do not refer to a "How to Ski" guide.

When truck drivers move down the highway, they do not refer to a "How to Drive" guide.

These skilled practitioners have learned what to do and they continue to refine their techniques. Let's look at some ways to apply processes in a fast-paced environment.

Training. Some roles require quick reactions, such as when a receptionist greets a visitor, when a downhill skier navigates an ice patch, or when a long-haul truck driver swerves to avoid an accident. The most effective workers are able to make quick decisions by instinct. But this ability was not acquired spontaneously. Everyone started as a beginner and then got better with the help of an instructor, coach, or on-the-job training. Instruction comes in many forms: mentorships, in-person demonstrations, classroom lectures, manuals, case studies, How-to Guides, online courses, simulations, and experiments.

Practice. Start with the basics and move up to more difficult processes. A former colleague loved the metaphor "crawl, walk, run." I think he used that phrase too often, but the principle is sound: master the basics before moving to advanced topics. Addition comes before algebra which comes before calculus.

Memorization. Use a mnemonic to remember key steps. For example, here are some ways that a truck driver can remember process steps:

- How should I inspect the tires? Remember ABC: Do you see any Abrasions, Bulges, or Cuts?
- How should I inspect the truck components? Remember CDL: is anything Cracked, Damaged, or Loose?
- How should I handle a difficult backing maneuver? Remember GOAL: Get Out And Look.

Analysis afterward. For processes that need to be performed from memory, you can combine training beforehand with analysis afterward. The U.S. Army uses an "after action report" to capture what went well and what went wrong after a military training exercise. In the heat of battle, quick action is needed based on extensive training. Afterward, they ask, "What can we do better?"

There are six phases to the throw of a baseball pitcher.[3] Each phase has several movements and subtleties distinguishing a good pitcher from a bad one. There is no pitching manual on the pitcher's mound, so when the count is 3-and-2, the pitcher doesn't consult pages 14 through 18 to review how to strike out the batter with a curveball. Instead, techniques and improvements must be mastered in practice. Coaches use video analysis to examine a player's pitching mechanics and provide specific advice on how to improve.

To help someone improve how they run a challenging process, use video, verbal recaps, or past results to explore what went well and what needs improvement.

Quick reference guides. I'm always impressed that when I ask for help finding something in a grocery store, the team member can point me to the correct aisle from memory. Where can I find a small can of diced green chile peppers? Aisle 9, midway down on the left side. Occasionally, when I ask someone for help, they need to refer to a store directory app on their phone. Accessing this quick reference guide takes just a few seconds, but then they know right where to point me. I'm glad they can look it up since it saves me from wandering around the store.

American football coaches use a large, laminated sheet to see all the possible play calls during a game. Using columns, tables, and lots of colors, they can see the full array of options available. Whether the scenario is "third and long" or "goal line with short yardage," the coaches have immediate access to the information they need.

Provide your team with quick access to the list they need. You could use a printed sheet, web page, laminated card, poster, or mobile app.

Technology. Wearable computers and heads-up displays provide access to information without using our hands. Tablets and touchscreens allow quick interactions with documents. Online forms can include instructions and validations that minimize bad data being input. Audio cues such as alarms, tones, and verbal warnings can prompt certain actions. Visual signals such as signs, arrows, and floor markings can aid with completing a process. Dashboards or status screens can provide real-time feedback.

Checklist for using your processes in day-to-day work

☐ Use How-to Guides at all levels in your organization.

☐ Organize your How-to Guides by functional area and make them easily accessible.

☐ Update or flag How-to Guides as you work. Remove ambiguity and note improvement opportunities.

☐ Capture variations and frustrations in writing.

☐ Use your existing software in a process-focused way. Add process management software to build and optimize your Process Library.

Chapter 11

How to Use Your Processes With Your Team

Identify	Describe	Use	Improve
Chapter 4. Identify Your **Functional Areas**		Chapter 10. Use Your Processes in **Day-to-Day Work**	Chapter 13. **Improve** Your Processes
Chapter 5. Identify Your **Roles**	Chapter 8. Describe Your Processes With **Attributes**	Chapter 11. Use Your Processes With **Your Team**	Chapter 14. Improve Your Processes by **Learning from Others**
Chapter 6. Identify Your **Processes**	Chapter 9. Describe Your Processes Using **How-To Guides**	Chapter 12. Use Your Processes With **Business Frameworks**	Chapter 15. Improve Your Processes Using **External Resources**
Chapter 7. Identify **Gaps and Opportunities**			

Nobody's an island. We depend on people inside and outside our organization to get things done. As we're running our own processes, we receive input from others and provide results to others. Whether we're the team leader or a team member, we need to find the best ways to work together by collaborating and delegating.

The Process Pilot (described in Chapter 5) should first identify and describe all their own processes. Their work becomes the basis for the next group of team leaders working on process improvement. Each team should build a culture of continuous improvement where everyone can identify, describe, use, and improve their processes.

The Process Prescription optimizes each team's performance by moving team leaders toward collaboration and away from isolation. Let's look at ways the Process Prescription can extend beyond an individual to your entire team.

Delegate with clarity

Delegation is itself a process. If you improve how you delegate to employees, contractors, and external companies, then work gets done with less stress and with more consistency.

How to delegate: avoid micromanagement

Micromanagement involves too much supervision and too little trust in people. Micromanagement is expensive. It requires managers to monitor people when they could be doing more valuable work. Micromanagers annoy skilled workers by treating them like untrustworthy children.

The Process Prescription is exactly the opposite of micromanagement. The Process Prescription overcomes the problems that micromanagement creates.

By agreeing on what's acceptable, managers won't need to look over the shoulders of their team members. People can solve their own problems and flourish as they capture troubleshooting techniques. Your team can accept the challenge of defining the best way to work. Once everyone agrees on standard methods, people are left alone to run their processes. Of course, they can still reach out for help, but their supervisor is not babying them.

The Process Prescription empowers people to describe, follow, and improve their processes.

In the software development projects I've led, I didn't tell the developers how to write each line of source code. However, we did need to agree on the following beforehand:

- How to collaborate with sprints (short work cycles) and weekly check-ins
- How to track and view the current priorities
- How to claim tasks from the backlog
- How to log bugs and feature requests
- How to store and update the source code
- How to test and release new versions

With those ground rules, the developers were free to innovate. Even a creative role like a software engineer needs processes for time management and collaboration. It would be a waste of their valuable time (and the company's cash) if every developer needed to invent new processes for all their supporting activities.

When I worked at McDonald's in high school, I cooked Big Macs and Quarter Pounders. After receiving training based on McDonald's exacting written standards, I understood the step-by-step processes. I did not need continual supervision. As a kitchen crew member, I knew the expectations and routines. Our team worked together to prepare the food according to the high standards set by the company. We also knew we could ask a manager if something unexpected happened that we didn't know how to handle.

How to delegate: consider what and how

You may say, "I care about results, not all the steps taken to get there. It's about what, not how. Spare me the details! Just get it done!"

But buried in those exhortations are assumptions you're making about the people doing the work. Namely,

1. They will follow local, state, and national laws.
2. They will uphold the values and mission of your organization.
3. They will not spend unlimited amounts of money.
4. They will follow the standards that you set.
5. They will not make stupid mistakes that subject you to unnecessary risks.
6. They will not take forever to accomplish the task.
7. They will work in a way that creates value and doesn't mess things up in the long run.

When you tell someone what you want, you care about how it's done. If you delegate to others without setting expectations, then the people doing the work have to guess or rely on unwritten rules to meet your standards. Instead, set and communicate your standards as part of a delegation process. You want to set clear criteria for success.

But how should those standards be set? Where along the continuum from too-hands-on to too-hands-off do you want to be? Are you a micromanager or a macro-manager? Either extreme can be harmful.

To find the right balance, adjust the level of detail in your How-to Guides based on your customers' needs, your team members' skills, and external factors such as regulatory requirements.

If your customers have particular needs related to quality or timeliness, your How-to Guides should include those specific expectations.

If your team members possess a core set of skills, your How-to Guides can provide instructions at a higher level. For example, a trained chef would know how to julienne carrots without needing step-by-step instructions.

If your business is subject to audits or inspections, ensure your How-to Guides include the exact standards and level of readiness required.

How to delegate: consider who and how

A variation of "what not how" is "who not how," which postulates that you should choose the right person for a job and let them work without interference. The right "who" will be able to do the job correctly without instructions. You don't need to micromanage the person you hire. You can delegate many "hows" (process steps) to one "who" (a competent person).

Dan Sullivan wrote a book about this: *Who Not How: The Formula to Achieve Bigger Goals Through Accelerating Teamwork.* Note the word "formula" in the title, which indicates that the book will include a step-by-step recipe for achieving the promised "bigger goals." One chapter is titled "How to Create Effective Collaborations." Despite its title, the book explains in great detail *how* to delegate by finding experts who can help you get things done.

Delegation is a powerful tool. But in practice, it's about who *and* how. You need to develop a repeatable process for delegation. Even if you want to engage in extreme delegation by paying others to complete as many of your tasks as possible, you still need a process for doing that.

To delegate effectively by converting some of your how's into who's, you'll need a process that covers the following:

- How to identify projects and functions that are suitable for outsourcing. Are you okay with losing expertise in the area you're outsourcing?
- How to find the right person to delegate to. Sources include referrals, agencies, and online marketplaces. Do you have a Plan B if the expert you hire needs to leave?
- How to interview and choose the right person or company. This includes validating a candidates' skills and determining if they're a fit.
- How to agree on satisfactory compensation. Is their price affordable, considering what it would cost you to do the same thing in-house? What if you find the right person, but they are too expensive?
- How to define the objectives, expectations, and success criteria for your project.

Free up your time and attention by delegating tasks that are not part of your business's core expertise. For example, a grocery store delegates its nightly floor cleaning. A manufacturer delegates its tax preparation.

Delegation works best when you follow a set of processes to collaborate with an external expert and build a high level of trust.

How to delegate: avoid "out of sight, out of mind"

You may think, "My business outsources that function, so I don't need a process." It's true that if you outsource a business function, you don't need to know about every detailed process in that area. That's the main idea behind outsourcing: it saves you the time and headache of running that area.

For example, my friend Ryan outsources his company's computer support to a Managed Services Provider (MSP). This is smart; he can focus on his core business and doesn't need to worry about setting up new email accounts, renewing domain names, or configuring the office network. But he does need to manage the ongoing outsourcing process. If there's a problem working with the MSP, then Ryan needs to fix it. In the worst case, he needs to find another MSP to help with his company's information technology needs.

Ryan could create a process named "How to work with our IT Managed Services Provider." This guide could answer the following:

- How do we find the best MSP for outsourcing our IT support?
- What should we look for in an MSP? What should we avoid?
- What are the exact processes that we have outsourced to them?
- What elements do we include in a Service Level Agreement? What happens if they don't meet the agreed-upon requirements?
- How do we renegotiate our contract with them? The more we know about what they do (and what they don't do), the more negotiating leverage we have.
- How do we review outsourced processes to make sure we're not paying for things we no longer need?
- How do we work with the MSP to make them as productive as possible?
- How do we evaluate the MSP's work? How do we check the completed output? What metrics should we use? How often

should we do this? How will mistakes and problems be resolved? Is the MSP committed to improving its processes?

- How do we record and resolve problems?
- How often do we meet with the MSP, even if there are no pressing concerns?

Even though Ryan outsources his technology support function, he still needs a process to ensure he's getting maximum value from the relationship.

If he creates an effective How-to Guide for outsourcing and managing IT support, then he can apply that to outsourcing other non-core areas of his business.

How to delegate: track 'who' and 'when' for a process

The process is what needs to be done, and the How-to Guide is how to do it. But who should use the How-to Guide, and when? You can clarify the who and the when by creating two views based on information in your Process Library.

First, create role descriptions. Sort the processes in your Process Library by the assigned roles. The list of all the processes assigned to a role creates a role description for that role. A role description becomes a personalized Operations Manual for the person who fills that role.

Second, create a shared calendar. Sort the processes in your Process Library by process frequency and due date. This shows when each process should be run. Refer to this calendar regularly to confirm that processes are being completed on time. Processes that are not scheduled should have a frequency of "as-needed" and won't appear on this calendar.

Use your shared calendar to generate tasks from recurring processes. Anticipate upcoming tasks and track the completion of those tasks. For example, an accountant has a process related to closing the general ledger each month. That parent process generates a monthly child task that needs to be completed each month.

You can use calendaring software or process management software to generate a list of recurring tasks based on the schedule for each process.

Clarify the benefits for your team

If your team is reluctant to create documentation for their processes, work to understand their underlying concerns. If your team doesn't want you to know what they're doing, then describe the benefits of sharing process knowledge. The Process Prescription does not just benefit the organization; the benefits accrue to individual team members, too.

How team members benefit: less risk

If someone is following an established process and there's a problem, the organization shares responsibility for the problem. But if someone working in isolation causes a problem, then they shoulder much of the blame. The Process Prescription helps us remember things so there are fewer errors and annoyances. When errors do occur, we can write down what happened and learn from the incident.

The Process Prescription removes the "single point of failure" risk that occurs when only one person knows how to perform a process. By applying the Process Prescription, a backup person can step into a role temporarily if there's an emergency or an absence.

The Process Prescription can uncover attempts to hide mistakes, ineffi- ciencies, corner-cutting, or nefarious activities. Even if just one person hides their activities, supervisors and colleagues can get dragged down by that person's negligence or wrongdoing. Adding transparency is key to finding potential problems before they explode.

How team members benefit: easier work

The Process Prescription makes work easier, faster, and more consistent. Team members have quick access to a Process Library with How-to Guides. Repetitive tasks get completed faster. Focus shifts to more interesting and challenging projects. The workload is more balanced, so there is less pressure to meet sudden deadlines. Things flow more smoothly.

How team members benefit: more learning and more opportunities

The Process Prescription leads to more opportunities to grow and advance their careers. Here are the learning opportunities the Process Prescription provides:

*   Team members learn how to improve the way they work. They learn to improve consistency, identify waste, lower costs, solve problems, and reduce frustration. They become innovators and improvement specialists.
*   Team members learn how to describe and explain what they do and to others. They become trainers, mentors, and advisers.
*   Team members learn new skills, tools, and techniques to support their current roles. They become experts.
*   Team members learn about other roles in your organization and how they work together. They become managers, facilitators, and collaborators.
*   Team members learn how processes interact. They become integrators and planners.
*   Team members learn how to measure success and growth. They become analysts and strategists.

Work becomes more interesting since visibility into how things work leads to innovation and improvement. With process visibility, team members can cross-train on multiple jobs making them more versatile and valuable.

Find and train new team members

As people leave your team and others join, you need processes for hiring and training. The Process Prescription helps prepare for change and minimize the disruption when someone leaves.

The Process Prescription allows you to save money when hiring new team members. If you only hire people who perfectly match an existing role in your business, this will be expensive. You can expect to spend substantial time and money on your recruiting process, since fewer "perfect matches" exist.

But what if you could find someone with intelligence, integrity, and initiative, and train them to fill a role and run their processes with excellence?[1]

Use this approach to expand your talent search. You can tap into new sources of talent and apply a process to help them learn and get up-to-speed quickly.

- Could the physics student who understands $e = mc^2$ also troubleshoot your computer network?
- Could the affable, healthy guy who sells gym memberships also sell cars?
- Could the detail-oriented receptionist also do some basic bookkeeping?
- Could a talented software engineer who knows one programming language also learn another language?
- Could a stay-at-home parent serve as a patient, attentive customer service rep?

Hire people with the 3 I's (intelligence, initiative, and integrity), and then use your How-to Guides to help them succeed. Once you hire a new person, use the Process Prescription to upgrade their skills. First, understand what the new person already knows. Next, identify what they need to know to run the processes assigned to them. Plan how they are going to acquire the needed knowledge and skills. Describe their onboarding and training process in a How-to Guide.

Someone who grows up in your organization and enjoys your unique culture of learning, innovating, and improving will be inclined to stay. Even if someone leaves before you'd like, you'll have plenty of options for finding and developing new talent.

Provide How-to Guides, training pathways, and checklists that allow your eager (but less-than-skilled) new hires to learn and run your processes. There is a risk they may soak up knowledge from you and then quit to join another organization. But in the meantime, you've refined your onboarding process which will stay with your company. You can apply that process again to your next hire. This process gives you a competitive advantage.

Protect intellectual property within your team

Everyone in your business does not need to know everything about your business. You need to keep some things secret. Personnel files are not open for public view. Past mistakes aren't posted in a public forum. Aspects of your finances or compensation may be known only within a small group.

And there are things you've created to make your company special and valuable, such as the following:

- Your trade secrets, recipes, and formulas
- Your method of interviewing prospective clients to understand their needs
- Your method of prioritizing new deals or opportunities
- Your technology, software, and related methods

Even these secret processes need to be documented so they're not lost or forgotten. You can control access to the secrets on a need-to-know basis.

Encourage innovation within your team

If you're concerned that the Process Prescription may stifle innovation, don't worry. The Process Prescription is not about stifling new ideas. It's about the opposite: accelerating and sustaining innovation.

An innovative chef creates a recipe that allows her to capture and preserve her creativity. After she develops and perfects a new menu item, she writes down how to prepare that entrée in a recipe. Now her sous chef and line cooks can make it, too.

An innovative, Nobel Prize-winning scientist uses the scientific method to structure experiments and lead an investigative team. The scientific method itself is a process: hypothesize, experiment, and validate.

Suppose an innovative writer follows a writing routine: he visits his favorite coffee shop and opens his favorite writing app on his favorite laptop. Does that process stifle innovation? Is he too formulaic? On the contrary, that comfortable routine allows him to focus on the creative aspects of his writing.

Once an idea is hatched, it can be cultivated with a process. Even if the initial spark of an idea occurs spontaneously, a process can develop that idea. You can nurture the kernel of an idea through the stages of validation, refinement, production, and testing.

Was Thomas Edison's realization that a filament could glow and provide light an innovation? That was not a new idea at the time. Edison's innovation was to improve an existing idea with his team in his laboratory. They worked diligently, trying thousands of options to find a better filament for the electric light. Edison explained that "genius is one percent inspiration and ninety-nine percent perspiration."[2]

Was Paul McCartney's innovation the three-note progression that came to him in a dream, sung to the words "scrambled eggs?" Or was it the process of refining that tune, writing lyrics, and working with a team to record the song "Yesterday?" After the inspiration occurred, it fed into a process that developed the idea into something far more valuable.

Support autonomy within your teams

Allow your teams the autonomy to experiment and find new ways of solving problems. But autonomy is not the same as isolation. Give your teams what they need to pursue creative solutions, including the following:

- Technology and Tools. What technology and tools does the team need to work quickly? Is there an existing platform or architecture that they can build on?
- Risk Guardrails. What risks are permissible, and what risks should be avoided?
- Objectives. What defines success? What are milestones along the way?

Address poor behavior within your team

As the Process Prescription identifies new opportunities, it also exposes counter-productive behavior that holds back your business. Let's look at three types of unhelpful team members that the Process Prescription reveals.

The Tyrant uses their specialized knowledge to control a particular area of the business. For example, a Tyrant in the accounting department could refuse to share how things work. Things get done on time, but other team members must rely on the Tyrant's guidance and approval. The Tyrant hoards knowledge to preserve manual processes, their favorite routines, their favorite vendors, and their high salary. Tyrants focus on what's best for themselves, not the organization.

The Goldbricker uses gold paint to make a worthless brick appear valuable. A goldbricker in your organization appears busy (externally they're golden), but they're not adding much value (internally they're brick).

The Statue likes things frozen in time. This isn't a comment about old people or young people. The Statue resists change, and this type of thinking can occur at any age. Statues are unwilling to adjust or improve the way they work.

Once you discover these people, decide if they can be retrained or placed in a role that fits their personality and preferences better. If not, they need to leave.

How to keep the momentum going

Once your team begins using How-to Guides, what's the best way to maintain the progress? Let's look at some ways your organization can keep things moving forward.

Conduct 1-to-1 meetings

Your team members can participate in scheduled meetings with their supervisor to share progress and receive feedback. In a 1-to-1 meeting, a supervisor meets individually with a team member and asks questions to find ways to provide support. The meeting could last 30 minutes or less and could be held weekly or less often, depending on what works best for your business. Create a process for "How to conduct a 1-to-1 meeting with a team member." Here are some possible topics for a 1-to-1 meeting:

- How are you doing?
- What process are you working to define or refine?
- What process needs better documentation?

- Can I provide any guidance for running or documenting your processes?
- Does any process need immediate troubleshooting?
- What annoyance can I help you resolve before it grows into a bigger problem?
- What process frustrates you, and why?
- What is the next step for resolving that?

A 1-to-1 meeting can also review each person's Objectives and Key Results, which can include process-related goals. Establishing 1-to-1 meetings as a core activity guides your team members, develops their skills, and helps them troubleshoot and improve their processes.

Set goals for improving processes

You can create a process improvement goal with a monthly or quarterly deadline. For example, suppose your Sales Manager has a reliable method for finding new prospects, but it's mostly in his head and, therefore, can't be easily shared. You could set a goal of having a draft version of that process written down before the end of the month. Set another goal for the next month to have a more detailed version that someone else could follow. The next month, have someone follow the new process and provide suggestions. This process goes from being undocumented to fully shareable and scalable within a few months. By adding new details each month, your team can level out the process documentation workload without the pressure to describe everything all at once. The result is steady improvement.

Use a morning meeting to identify challenges

Some companies use a morning meetings to educate and inspire their team. Ten to twenty minutes is enough time for learning, encouragement, and team-building. Team members can rotate the responsibility for leading the meeting so everyone can develop presentation skills. Despite the time cost, this develops a culture of sharing where everyone helps each other to learn and grow.

Checklist for using your processes with your team

☐ Develop and implement a roll-out plan with your Process Architect and Process Pilot(s). Resolve problems quickly.

☐ Delegate processes to free up time, but provide clear expectations and use How-to Guides.

☐ Communicate how the Process Prescription provides direct benefits to your team.

☐ Set standards for cooperation and teamwork. Don't let poor behavior persist.

☐ Create routines that make collaboration easier, such as 1-to-1 meetings, morning meetings, and quarterly goals.

Chapter 12

How to Use Your Processes With Business Frameworks

Identify	Describe	Use	Improve
Chapter 4. Identify Your **Functional Areas**		Chapter 10. Use Your Processes in **Day-to-Day Work**	Chapter 13. **Improve** Your Processes
Chapter 5. Identify Your **Roles**	Chapter 8. Describe Your Processes With **Attributes**	Chapter 11. Use Your Processes With **Your Team**	Chapter 14. Improve Your Processes by **Learning from Others**
Chapter 6. Identify Your **Processes**	Chapter 9. Describe Your Processes Using **How-To Guides**	Chapter 12. Use Your Processes With **Business Frameworks**	Chapter 15. Improve Your Processes Using **External Resources**
Chapter 7. Identify **Gaps and Opportunities**			

You can combine the Process Prescription with other helpful frameworks for organizing and improving your business. A business framework consists of essential elements or techniques that serve as a pattern for success. The four-step Process Prescription (Identify - Describe - Use - Improve) is itself a framework that can complement and enhance other frameworks.

The Process Prescription can co-exist with a variety of different management and business-building approaches. Any framework that involves describing processes can benefit from the Process Prescription. Let's look at some business frameworks in two categories: functional and whole-organization.

Functional frameworks

Functional frameworks help describe and organize one particular area of your business. You can boost the effectiveness of a functional framework by combining it with the Process Prescription and How-to Guides.

For marketing executives, the 5 P's of Marketing (Product, Price, Promotion, Place, and People) provide a well-rounded view of the possible levers for getting results. The Process Prescription and How-to Guides can detail how each 'P' is implemented within your organization.

For auditors, the Segregation of Duties (SOD) approach helps prevent fraud and mismanagement. The Process Prescription and How-to Guides can explain how your organization assigns the responsibilities related to SOD.

For accountants in the United States, Generally Accepted Accounting Principles (GAAP) detail the standards for reporting financial results. The Process Prescription and How-to Guides can describe how those rules are applied to your organization.

For technology leaders, the IT Infrastructure Library (ITIL) describes best practices for delivering IT services. The Process Prescription and How-to Guides can describe the right way to use those standards in your environment.

For manufacturers, Statistical Process Control (SPC) techniques help track consistency and identify troublesome trends. The Process Prescription and How-to Guides can describe when and how to apply SPC in your business.

Whole-Organization Frameworks

In addition to functional frameworks, there are business frameworks that can apply to any type of business. These frameworks apply to your entire organization and extend to all areas and levels, not just one department. The Process Prescription is a whole-organization framework since it applies to all areas of your business by describing who should do what, when, and how.

You can combine the Process Prescription with any business framework to create a "business operating system" customized for your organization.

Let's look at how the Process Prescription complements some popular business frameworks.

Toyota Production System

Jeffrey Liker's book *The Toyota Way: 14 Management Principles from the World's Greatest Manufacturer* describes effective automotive production methods developed by Taiichi Ohno at Toyota Motor Company. The principles of *The Toyota Way* can be lived out using the Process Prescription. For example, How-to Guides for applying this approach could include the following:

- How to level out the workload (heijunka)
- How to use visual controls to identify problems early
- How to use "pull" systems to avoid overproduction
- How to identify and eliminate waste

You can distill the wisdom of Toyota's management principles into How-to Guides with actionable steps.

Rockefeller Habits

In his book *Mastering the Rockefeller Habits: What You Must Do to Increase the Value of Your Growing Firm*, Vern Harnish describes habits related to communication, gathering input, planning, setting goals, and analysis.[1]

You can put Harnish's habits into practice using the Process Prescription and How-to Guides. Planning and analysis are both focus areas that appear as rows on the Process Matrix. Setting goals is a strategy process, which should appear in the top row of your Process Matrix.

The Learning Organization

Peter Senge's book *The Fifth Discipline: The Art and Practice of the Learning Organization*[2] describes a learning organization as a place "where people continually expand their capacity to create the results they truly desire, where new and expansive patterns of thinking are nurtured, where collective aspiration is set free, and where people are continually learning how to learn together."[3]

To achieve these ends, Senge suggests using five "component technologies":

- Systems thinking
- Personal mastery
- Mental models
- Shared vision
- Team learning

Senge's "system thinking" can be implemented using the Process Prescription and How-to Guides.

Entrepreneurial Operating System ®

Gino Wickman's book *Traction: Get a Grip on Your Business* lists six key components for any business: Vision, Data, Process, Traction, Issues, and People.[4] These components form the basis for the concept of an "Entrepreneurial Operating System," or EOS.

Each of Wickman's components can be implemented using the Process Prescription and How-to Guides as follows:

- Vision can be cast by leadership and preserved using processes in the strategy row of the Process Matrix.

- Data relates to processes, either as an input or an output. Data gaps can be flagged for future analysis.
- Process identification and improvement are completely in sync with the Process Prescription.
- Traction in your business is achieved when processes run consistently and generate value. You can create processes to measure and accelerate your progress.
- Issues can be flagged and linked to their underlying process. Recurring problems can be resolved using the "people or process?" approach.
- People first. The Process Prescription prioritizes the people who run the processes by valuing their input and ideas.

The E-Myth

Michael Gerber's book *The E-Myth Revisited: Why Most Small Businesses Don't Work and What to Do About It*[5] lists seven centers of management attention:

- Leadership
- Marketing
- Money
- Management
- Lead Conversion
- Lead Generation
- Client Fulfillment

These seven topics are similar to functional areas. Gerber describes "Action Plans" for each area which are equivalent to How-to Guides.

The 3 P's of Business

On each episode of the reality television show *The Profit*, Marcus Lemonis decides if he wants to invest in a struggling business. He sizes up the current situation, pinpoints challenges, and identifies solutions based on the Three P's: People, Process, and Product.[6] Marcus teaches business owners to develop processes and stick to them. He encourages teams to "trust the process" for clarifying expectations, improving quality, and replicating success. Applying the Process Prescription and using How-to Guides is an effective way to develop processes you can trust.

The 7-S Framework

McKinsey & Company, the global management consultancy, developed the 7-S framework in the 1970s. The framework describes how organizations can succeed by aligning and coordinating seven internal elements: Strategy, Structures, Systems, Shared Values, Skills, Style, and Staff.

McKinsey's "Systems" element can be implemented using the Process Prescription and How-to Guides. The Process Prescription can also help with the other six S's as they are described, taught, and learned.[7]

Work the System

In his book, *Work the System: The Simple Mechanics of Making More and Working Less*, Sam Carpenter tells the story of how he went from a stressed-out, struggling entrepreneur to a calm, strategic business owner by developing a collection of systems. Sam describes the need to have a systems mindset and to develop a "business machine" that runs without the owner being involved in everything.[8]

Organize and share the systems and working procedures that Sam describes using the Process Prescription and How-to Guides.

2 Second Lean

This approach to developing a lean culture is described in Paul Akers's book *2 Second Lean: How to Grow People and Build a Fun Lean Culture at Work and at Home*.[9]

The book's title comes from a question anyone can ask, "What improvement can I make that saves two seconds?" If everyone in your organization hunts for new ways to save time, then your operations become faster and better.

Paul recommends several specific techniques to streamline your business, including holding a morning meeting, having a place for everything, and creating videos to share your progress and methods.

One company that implemented 2 Second Lean began using these processes:

- How to create a learning club
- How to conduct a morning meeting, which includes sharing process learning and before-and-after photos
- How to use collaboration software to share ideas
- How to maintain a lean (and clean!) restroom
- How to create a "lean cave" with tools and materials
- How to organize a workspace using 3-S (Sweep, Sort, Standardize)
- How to look for problems
- How to participate as a leader on the shop floor

Capture and refine your methods for developing a growing lean business using the Process Prescription and How-to Guides.

Objectives and Key Results (OKRs)

John Doerr's book *Measure What Matters: How Google, Bono, and the Gates Foundation Rock the World with OKRs* describes a system of "management by objectives" developed by Andy Grove at Intel Corporation.[10]

This approach centers around answering a few key questions:

1. How do we know where we're going? This involves defining and refining our Mission and Vision.
2. How will we know how we're doing? This involves tracking Objectives and Key Results (OKRs) for groups and individuals.
3. How do we stay healthy along the way? This involves creating a culture of learning and improving.

This approach is highly compatible with the Process Prescription since you can develop processes to create, update, and track your OKRs. Capture your organization's entire OKR methodology in How-to Guides.

You can use OKRs to set goals for process creation and refinement.

Checklist for using your processes with business frameworks

☐ Look for published methods, checklists, and ideas from your peers and industry leaders. Refer to these processes and concepts when creating your How-to Guides.

☐ Adapt general principles and industry "best practices" into How-to Guides that are tailored for your organization.

☐ Create How-to Guides for developing and communicating vision, values, and culture. Use How-to Guides to explain concepts and implement strategies.

☐ When using a whole-organization framework, use the Process Prescrip tion to implement the process or systems component.

Chapter 13

How to Improve Your Processes

Identify	Describe	Use	Improve
Chapter 4. Identify Your **Functional Areas**	Chapter 8. Describe Your Processes With **Attributes**	Chapter 10. Use Your Processes in **Day-to-Day Work**	Chapter 13. **Improve** Your Processes
Chapter 5. Identify Your **Roles**		Chapter 11. Use Your Processes With **Your Team**	Chapter 14. Improve Your Processes by **Learning from Others**
Chapter 6. Identify Your **Processes**	Chapter 9. Describe Your Processes Using **How-To Guides**	Chapter 12. Use Your Processes With **Business Frameworks**	Chapter 15. Improve Your Processes Using **External Resources**
Chapter 7. Identify **Gaps and Opportunities**			

Google the term "Process Improvement," and you'll find more than a billion results. Entire categories of software exist to help with improving processes. Tens of thousands of pages have been written on this topic.

So how do you decide the best way to improve your processes? In this chapter, we look at some specific ways to prioritize and get started.

After following the steps in the Process Prescription, you've identified, described, and used your processes. You have collected your processes in a Process Library. You have a thorough, 360-degree view of your organization. Your business has had the equivalent of a head-to-toe physical exam, complete with an MRI and blood work. You have plenty of process information to work with.

According to manufacturing expert Shigeo Shingo, "There are four purposes of improvement: easier, better, faster, and cheaper. These four goals appear in the order of priority."[1]

To achieve these improvement goals, analyze your processes across various dimensions to find things worth improving. Look for the following:

- Usage patterns to streamline
- Similarities to combine or standardize
- Gaps to fill
- Inefficiencies to eliminate
- Growth constraints to loosen
- Error-prone processes to correct
- Ways to encourage innovation
- Ideas for applying different tools and methods

Resist the temptation to skip the first three steps of the Process Prescription (Identify, Describe, Use) and jump straight into this improvement phase. It's wiser to first take stock of the full set of your processes. Of course, stop any bleeding related to process emergencies, but don't get too far into the Improve phase without having completed the Identify, Describe, and Use phases.

This chapter provides an overview of several ways to improve your processes. As you find methods that fit your organization, apply them across your functional areas and explore them in more depth to develop your own expertise.

How to improve: refine your How-to Guides

The clarity and usefulness of your How-to Guides should continue to improve as your team uses them to run their processes. In Chapter 10, we looked at how to update your How-to Guides during your day-to-day work.

Let's look at some additional techniques to improve your How-to Guides.

Add if-then statements to your processes

The ability to self-correct is a valuable skill. When a problem occurs, your team members need to figure out alternatives and solutions. You don't want them to freeze with uncertainty. Building a feedback loop into your How-to Guides, will build a resilient, anti-fragile process that can respond to many different variations. For example,

- "If the machine gets stuck, then check and adjust these parts."
- "If you see this pattern, then take these precautions."
- "If you see this error message, then check these related systems."

Chain together these if-then statements to form a troubleshooting guide. When you see a problem, check one thing and then another in the specified order to determine the cause of the problem. Once you have discovered the cause, pick the best solution.

Record your mistakes

Write down every mistake that you make when running a process. Also, write down how you corrected the mistake and how it could be prevented in the future. Give people the freedom to report mistakes, even if something is their fault. Your organization will suffer if your team members hide their mistakes instead of sharing and learning from them.

"Fool me once, shame on you... fool me twice, shame on me." Write down each problem that occurs and find the root cause to minimize the chance of a recurrence. Don't get fooled twice by the same problem.

Football coach Jimbo Fisher puts it this way: "If you don't understand why you win or have success, it's wasted. If you don't understand why you make a mistake, why you do it, it's wasted."[3]

A manager at Lexus in Japan had this to say about mistakes: "You must smile when you find the defect. Because now you are closer to solving your problems."[5]

Even if a mistake was difficult or impossible to foresee, find the root cause. Also, consider contributing causes that made the mistake more likely, failed to prevent the mistake, or worsen the outcome. Once you understand the causes, take corrective action to prevent that sequence of events from happening again. You can also take precautions to reduce the loss if the mistake happens again.

If the problem is periodic and unavoidable, such as a tornado in Oklahoma or a hurricane in Miami, then write down in advance how you will handle the problem, minimize damage, and recover.

If you capture errors as you use your How-to Guides, you can examine that data for patterns and improvement opportunities.

I use this approach in my How-to Guide for a lengthy report that I create each month.

At each step where something could go wrong in the process, I make notes about how to avoid problems and resolve them quickly if they occur. For each potential problem, I record how to do three things:

1. Identify. How to know if I have this problem? Do I see an error message, or should I look for a warning sign or malformed output?
2. Understand. What are the possible causes of this? How can I find the root cause of the problem? How do I create a list of possible causes?
3. Fix. How do I fix this problem? If I can't resolve it myself, who can I contact for help? What are emergency measures that I might need to take?

Once while generating this report, I got an error due to a missing software module. I had also seen this same error four years earlier. In my notes for how to troubleshoot this report, I had written "DEBUG: June 1, 20YY", followed by a description of what I had seen and how I fixed it four years ago. This fix involved multiple steps:

- Knowing where to download the missing software module
- Knowing how to install some required prerequisite software (which was a "problem within a problem" that had to be resolved)
- Knowing how to install the missing module.

Thankfully, the fix from four years earlier still worked, and I was able to solve the problem quickly and keep moving.

Even if the fix had not worked, I still would have had a written starting point to begin my troubleshooting. Don't let your valuable "how to fix it" knowledge go to waste. Capture this information within your How-to Guides. Create a "Troubleshooting" or "Debug" section in your How-to Guides. Place these sections near the steps where problems are likely to occur.

The only problems that take too much long are those that have not happened before.

Record your experiments

As you try different ways to improve your processes, write down what you've tried and how well it worked. Even if an experiment fails, that's useful information since you know what not to try again. Also, a failed experiment can inspire a different experiment that produces better results. After completing an experiment, write down ideas for what you could try next time or how the experiment could be improved in the future.

Use the Five Whys to find the root cause

When you encounter a problem or process failure, you can ask, "Why did that happen?" Then ask "Why?" again about your answer. Repeat this five times (approximately), and you can find the root cause. If you prevent the root cause, you stop the chain reaction that results in the failure.

Here's an example of how the Five Whys could be applied to the problem of a customer receiving a broken product.

- Why did that happen? The product was broken during shipment.

- Why? The packaging was not sufficient to protect the product during shipment.
- Why? Our shipping department used too little padding and a box that was too small.
- Why? We were running low on padding, and we ran out of the larger-sized box.
- Why? We did not reorder enough packaging supplies after an unexpectedly busy week last week.
- Why? We order the same amount every time without checking the stock level before ordering.
- Why? It takes too long to see how much packaging material we have left.
- Why? The packing materials are scattered, messy, and not easy to count.
- Why? We don't take the time each day to tidy our workspace.

Based on these questions, we've found some possible root causes: 1) lack of packing supplies and 2) sloppiness that makes it difficult to count the packing supplies on hand.

A poor solution would be to tell the shipping clerk to "Do better next time!" A more helpful solution would be to aim at preventing the root causes. For example, you could create or refine the following processes:

- How to order packing supplies. Include instructions for how to measure the current inventory of supplies. Or even simpler, add a yellow card among the supplies that shows up when it's time to re-order.
- How to tidy the shipping department. Include a checklist for what needs to be done and a photo of what a clean workspace looks like.

Use the "people or process?" diagnostic

When something bad happens, ask, "Was this a people problem or a process problem?"

A people problem occurs when a process exists that would have prevented the problem, but someone didn't follow the process. The solution for a people problem is to find out why they didn't follow the process and take corrective action. Was it due to a lack of training or a lack of skill? Was the task too difficult? Or was it due to tiredness, apathy, carelessness, or malicious intent? Each of those causes can have a different solution. Work on ways to prevent each cause.

A process problem occurs when a process is missing or when the existing process is inadequate. Even if someone wanted to complete the process the correct way, there was no step-by-step guide that would have prevented the problem. The solution to a process problem is to create a How-to Guide or fix the existing How-to Guide.

Use the diagnostic, "Process problem or people problem?" as a quick way to start improving your processes.

Find small improvements

When running a process, consider it a challenge to find ways to improve that process. Can you save just two seconds? This is the concept that Paul Akers explores in his book *2 Second Lean*.

If you save just two seconds by improving a process, that saves five hours per year if five people run that process five times per day.

Or, as George Washington said, "Many mickles make a muckle."[2] I think that translates into modern English as "many nickels make a buck."

Write down questions

Write down every question that anyone asks about a process. These questions could come up when someone is learning the process for the first time or when someone is interacting with the process. These questions will help you find out what needs clarification. If the person asking the question is lazy or inattentive, the problem may lie with that person. But an earnest question allows you to find something that needs a better explanation. Capture these questions (and the answers) to create a knowledgebase that will help those who run this process in the future.

The world's leading software companies collect questions and answers in a knowledgebase that they publish on their website. Everyone has access to the full set of questions that have already been asked and answered about how to use and troubleshoot their software. This approach allows many people to benefit from a single answer.

We can also capture questions at sales presentations, demos, webinars, and customer events. If you write down everything anyone asks, you can use those questions and answers to refine your presentation content for next time.

Create a results log

As you run a process, note any hiccups or anomalies that differ from the standard How-to Guide. After you complete a process, make a note of the result and whether you encountered any problems. Add photos or videos if needed. Such a results log is useful when you want to review what went well and what needs improvement. Sports teams use "game film" to study their performance and see how well they ran their processes (plays) and how their opponents responded.

In the words of Taiichi Onho, the founder of the Toyota Production System, said, "The workplace is a teacher. You can find answers only in the workplace." Be a student of your workplace: observe, take notes, ask questions, learn, and improve.[4]

Look for steps to eliminate

Are there steps in a process that could be skipped without any negative impact? For example,

- Are you creating copies of files that are already safely stored elsewhere?
- Are you waiting for verification, feedback, or approval on inconsequential items?
- Are you notifying people of things that they never act on?
- Are you creating reports that nobody reads?
- Are you sending things to people instead of letting them come and get what they need?

Track duration

How long does it take you to complete a process? As you work on a process, write down the start time, stop time, and duration. Record the time for any process lasting more than a few minutes. Does the amount of time to run the process vary? If so, why? What makes it faster or slower? What's the slowest part? What could speed that up? Do you need to change the amount of time allocated to complete a process?

How to improve: embrace lean thinking and eliminate waste

Principles from the Toyota Production System (TPS) have been embraced by many companies, and the concepts have been genericized as lean manufacturing or lean production. The broader term *lean thinking* refers to the set of lean concepts that can apply to all types of organizations, not just manufacturers. These concepts include identifying the value-creating steps of a process, making sure these steps flow together, and minimizing waste.

A core part of lean thinking is a focus on eliminating waste. The Eight Wastes of Lean can be remembered using the acronym TIMWOODS: transportation, inventory, motion, waiting, over-production, over-processing, defects, and skills.

One waste can lead to another: overproduction waste results in wasteful transportation to move the excess production to inventory. Inventory can become damaged or defective, which leads to excess motion and over-processing to fix things. Meanwhile, the customer waits, and human potential and skills are wasted.

With some practice, you can spot these wastes as you see things being made, moved, and stored. Identifying waste is more straightforward in a manufacturing setting where you can see people working or not working and see things moving or not moving.

These wastes are more difficult to see in an office environment since much of the work involves files, messages, and applications moving on a screen, not on a factory floor. Let's look at some ways that the Eight Wastes can appear in a service-oriented or information-based business. If you work with physical products and equipment, you can still apply these ideas alongside the visible wastes you spot in your business.

Transportation

Transportation waste refers to the movement of things and information. We'll cover the wasted movement of people later under the waste of motion. Here are some examples of transportation waste in an office setting:

- Attaching something to an email instead of sharing a link or referring to a shared folder
- Sending an email instead of using a discussion thread in your collaboration software
- Sharing a paper document instead of a digital one
- Filing multiple copies of the same thing

Paper and email are common sources of transportation waste. These can often be eliminated using software and a better workflow. If you tag all your processes that use paper or email, you will generate plenty of ideas for improvement.

Inventory

Inventory waste refers to inputs or outputs stored for later use. In manufacturing, this waste applies to both raw materials inventory and finished goods. In an office, inventory could be information waiting to be processed or a backlog of tasks.

It costs time and money to acquire inventory. It takes time and energy to receive and organize the inventory. It takes space to store the inventory. More time is wasted retrieving an item from inventory. Plus, inventory can become obsolete, unneeded, damaged, lost, or stolen. All these problems with inventory apply to *both* physical things and digital files. The time spent searching for a digital file is just as costly as searching for a part in a warehouse.

Fundamentally, all inventory wastes our time and space, so we should work to minimize it. Examples of inventory waste include the following:

- Creating printouts or PDFs that need to be filed
- Maintaining a backlog of items to be tested, reviewed, or completed
- Holding requests or messages that need processing, replies, or approval
- Paying for unused software licenses
- Preserving archives or files longer than needed
- Delaying work until you have a big batch
- Owning supplies that are not being used. If you can reliably receive a supply shipment in two days, then you should not have more than two days' worth of supplies on hand. The advantages of a "bulk discount" can be offset by higher storage and spoilage costs.

Motion

The waste of motion refers to the unnecessary movement of people. To minimize this waste, look for ways to reduce the time and distance that people travel.

- Instead of making multiple trips to fetch supplies, use a checklist to assemble a kit with everything you need.
- Instead of bending down to reach something, place objects at a convenient height.
- Instead of conducting an in-person status meeting, post updates to a shared document.
- Instead of walking to use a machine, send the input electronically. Or move the machine closer to you. Or get your own machine.
- Instead of requiring an in-person demonstration, use video.
- Instead of re-typing data, automate data collection and sharing.
- Instead of scrolling up-and-down or side-to-side on a screen to find what you need, put the most frequently used information at the top of the page.

- Instead of walking around to identify problems, use lights, alerts, and dashboards.

Let's look at an activity that can waste a lot of motion: checking to see which team members have completed a required task. You may need to answer questions like the following:

- Has everyone completed the required training and assessment?
- Has everyone submitted the required form?
- Has everyone paid their fee?

Consider this manual method of checking who's completed a task.

1. Get the list of who *should* complete the task
2. Get the list of who *has* completed the task.
3. Compare the two lists by placing them side-by-side. Move down the "should do" list, making a note of who's not on the "has done" list.
4. Create a new list of the people who have not completed the task.
5. Send a follow-up reminder to the people who have not completed the task.
6. Repeat this process again later to see who still has not completed the task. Repeat until everyone completes the task.

All this activity of gathering, comparing, and reminding is wasteful. Instead, use software to track completion and send reminders.

Waiting

The waste of waiting occurs when I'm waiting for someone else to finish their work, which in turn is an input for my work. Here are some examples:

- Waiting for someone to approve my expense report
- Waiting for someone to respond with a decision
- Waiting for someone to set a date or schedule an event
- Waiting for someone to give me data so that I can do the analysis
- Waiting for someone to fill out a form

To minimize waiting, ask these questions:

- Does the person I'm waiting on have all the information and materials required? If not, how can I help them get what they need?
- Can we agree on a schedule for them to do the work or provide a response?
- Can anything be automated?
- Can anything be eliminated or rearranged to allow faster processing?
- Can anything be pre-processed to help complete the work faster?
- Can I get pre-approval as long as certain criteria are met?

Over-production

Those who overproduce tend to believe that "if a little is good, a lot must be better." Making too much spawns other problems, such as wasted transportation, wasted motion, and inventory. Examples of "too much" and "too many" include the following:

- Too much information, such as creating reports that nobody reads.
- Too many meetings
  - Creating in-person training or classwork, but the learning could be done by reading, watching a video, or taking an online course.
  - Having daily meetings when a weekly meeting would suffice.
  - Holding a long meeting when a shorter one would get the same results.
  - Requiring too many people to attend a meeting.
  - Having a meeting to collect feedback, but everyone could simply update their progress using collaboration software.
- Too many services
  - Subscribing to multiple software packages that do nearly the same thing.
  - Paying for backups or security measures that are not needed.
- Too much office

- ○ Having more luxurious office space than you need or decorating your office to impress customers, but customers never visit.
- ○ Having desks or areas that are unused.
- Too much insurance
  - ○ Buying a lot of insurance, but you are able to self-insure for all or part of a loss. Maintaining a deductible that is too low.
- Too many supplies
  - ○ Ordering marketing materials and promotional items that get stale too soon.
  - ○ Buying the same supplies or tools for everyone, including things that not everyone needs or wants.

Over-processing

Over-processing waste occurs when you do a job too thoroughly. You only need to do what the customer expects and is willing to pay for. We can look to home construction for an example of this. There are six levels of drywall finishing, from Level 0 to Level 5.[6.] The higher the level, the smoother the wall. If the wall is going to be covered with tile, you can stop at Level 2. If the wall is going to be covered with a heavy texture, you only need Level 3. If the wall will be painted and needs a super-smooth finish, exert the effort for Level 5. But don't waste your time and money on Level 5 if a lower level is sufficient.

Here are examples of over-processing:
- Offering too much customization
  - ○ Recreating a recurring email message from scratch every time instead of using a template.
  - ○ Giving your customers too much personalized attention. You can spend an infinite amount of money pursuing more customer happiness, so you need to know when "enough is enough."
- Gathering and providing too much information
  - ○ Using a printout when an online document would work.

- Creating an expensive, handcrafted prototype to gather feedback instead of using a 3D-printed version of the same item.
- Requiring too many approvals.
- Sending multiple messages instead of consolidating them into a single update.
- Providing status updates too often.
- Using a form that collects too much information, such as a physical mailing address, that you never intend to mail anything to.
- Being too helpful
  - Reminding people too many times to do something.
  - Providing the same level of service to every customer, even if they don't need it or want it.
  - Providing answers to questions that nobody has asked and nobody wants to know the answer to.
  - Providing too many product features beyond what a customer will pay extra for. This includes spending time on a project or assignment after you've already met the customer's requirements.

Identify where you are over-processing and eliminate those processes or process steps. Waste can also include an entire process. Do you run a process, but nobody uses the output? If so, get rid of the whole process.

Defects

For a manufactured product, a defect could refer to a loose part, a scratch, or a bad paint job. In an office setting, defects are less tangible, but you can spot them if you know where to look. Examples include the following:

- Delivering a message or report with a typo, incorrect date, misspelling, bad link, or inaccurate information.
- Releasing software with obvious bugs.
- Publishing an event reminder that fails to provide basic information about the date, time, location, and how to get there.

- Explaining something in a way that is not readily understandable.
- Leaving basic questions unanswered on your website. Some companies omit pricing information for their standard, well-defined products. I view this practice as annoying and defective.
- Providing instructions that are incomplete or inaccurate.

Make a note of defects as they occur and link these notes to the corresponding process. Create another process to find the cause of these defects. Implement a solution that will prevent or minimize a recurrence.

Skills not used

When your team's ideas and expertise are not used, you're wasting their skills. If your team members have useful input, but you ignore it, then that's disrespectful to them. You can extend this concept to include your customers; don't waste their input, either.

Examples of wasted skills include the following:

- Not having a system to collect ideas and suggestions from your team members, volunteers, customers, and partners.
- Not understanding all the skills and abilities of your team members, leadership, and board members.
- Not reviewing and considering the suggestions and ideas that you receive.
- Not having a pathway for your team members to learn, develop their abilities, and pursue their professional interests.

To avoid these wastes, develop processes to tap into the full potential of your team, such as the following:

- How to set up and maintain a form to collect suggestions
- How to conduct a skills inventory
- How to conduct and process a survey of your team members
- How to create a learning plan for professional development

I recently needed help with some software that wasn't behaving as expected. I used the software company's online chat feature to get technical support. After the chat, I got a survey with one question: "How easy was it to get the help you needed?" and five possible answers: one star to five stars.

After I provided a rating, there was one follow-up question: "Any comments you wish to add?"

That's a simple, effective approach to gathering feedback. The second question provided an easy way for me, the customer, to provide a suggestion. Some customers may choose to skip the question or unleash an unhelpful rant, but others may have some useful input. You don't know until you ask.

Another powerful technique for collecting ideas is to ask just these two questions:

- "On a scale of 1 (low) to 4 (high), how satisfied are you with our product or service?"
- "What works well or needs improvement?"

Asking these two questions will produce a lot of useful feedback. You don't need to ask about each and every product feature and possible concern since anything that's significant will prompt a comment.

A Ninth Waste?

In some situations, people have suggested adding another type of waste to the list of Eight Wastes. Ideas for a Ninth Waste have included the following:

- Knowledge. This is when the know-how and process intelligence from your team is not captured and shared. I think this waste is already covered by "Skills not shared."
- Over-thinking. This is when you fall victim to "analysis paralysis" and spend too much time looking at too many options rather than pursuing a path forward. I think this waste is included in the waste of over-processing. If customers aren't paying you to weigh every possibility in your mind, and there's an acceptable option already available, then such overthinking is a form of waste.
- Communication (or Lack of Communication). This is when someone is missing information about a process. I think this waste manifests as some of the other wastes:

- ◦ If someone needs more information before proceeding, this results in waiting and wasted time. This can also result in transportation waste when a request must be sent to get an update.
- ◦ If work stacks up because someone needs more information, this results in inventory waste.
- ◦ If people have to move to check the status of something, this wastes motion.

Since these proposed wastes fall within one or more of the Eight Wastes, I'm not convinced that we need to add a ninth waste to the list.

How to improve: use other lean thinking tools

In this section, we'll look at more *lean thinking* concepts that can benefit your organization.

Several of these lean concepts have Japanese names. By using the Japanese name, we're reminded of the subtitles and finer points of the concept behind each word. Some terms like *kaizen* and *kanban* are popular enough to have entered the English lexicon.

The 5-S's

The five S's are Sort, Set in Order, Shine, Standardize, and Sustain. These are different aspects of keeping your workspace tidy and clean for maximum productivity. Not only are you able to find things faster, you can also put things away quickly and save space since junk is not piled everywhere. Paul Akers shortens 5-S to 3-S (Sweep, Sort, and Standardize), which I think is a helpful simplification and makes this concept even easier to remember.[7]

Heijunka

This Japanese concept (pronounced hey-june-kuh) translates as "evenness" or "leveling." Try to avoid feast-or-famine in terms of your workload. Strive for a level, consistent volume of work.

- If you have a variety of tasks with different durations, choose a mix of tasks to level out the total amount of work each day.
- If two people have wildly different amounts of work, split each person's work into two parts and share the work evenly by having each person do half of the other person's work.
- If the daily demand for your work varies, but the weekly demand is consistent, do the average amount of work each day to meet the weekly demand.
- If you have unavoidable peak times or peak seasons (such as an accounting firm at tax time or a food truck at lunchtime), do as much preparation as possible. Make sure each team member's skills are flexible so that everyone can help during peak times.

Applying heijunka allows you to balance the workload fairly, plan work schedules, and avoid burnout. You can also provide clear expectations for productivity based on the amount of work that should be completed per day.

Another principle of heijunka is to avoid accumulating work into a big batch. Instead, work at a steady cadence and have people switch between tasks to match the demand. If your team can adapt to complete tasks at nearly the same pace that they're being requested, then you have less inventory waste and happier customers.

At the grocery store Trader Joe's, they know how to keep the checkout experience even and level. When there are too many customers in line, they ring a bell. This notifies team members in other parts of the store to open more checkout lanes. Instead of forcing customers to wait in a long queue, they open new lanes to keep things flowing smoothly.

Just-in-time

Just-in-time is one of the pillars of lean thinking and is facilitated by heijunka. Just-in-time has two aspects: pull and continuous flow. Pull occurs when workers can retrieve more work whenever they want instead of having to wait for a new task to be assigned. Continuous flow is when the work is being done (or the product being produced) at the same rate that the output is demanded by the customer. Generate a steady pace of work without the inconsistent pattern of starting, stopping, waiting, and resuming.

The opposite of just-in-time is working with large batches. Avoid large batches. A batch of work ties up money and time since the entire batch must be completed before the output is ready. Also, errors and production problems affect the whole batch rather than just the current item being worked on. Fixes have to be applied to many items rather than just one. People are more productive using just-in-time since they are not waiting for an upstream batch to finish before they can begin work. By applying just-in-time, you also spend less money on inventory and storage.

Standard Work

Creating standard processes and ways of doing things is a core part of the Process Prescription. This concept is also a key component of lean thinking. Find and document the best way to do something. Agree on the required output. Remove the burden and struggle of having to remember how to complete a process the right way.

Kaizen

The Japanese word *kaizen* means "change for the better." This idea is also referred to as "continuous improvement." The concept is that you should find ways to improve through conscious, deliberate effort. Your motivation to improve should stem from being a wise steward of the opportunities that you identify. Even a small improvement each week compounds into a much larger change over a year.

Kanban

Kanban (pronounced kahn-bahn) means "sign" or "billboard." Sharing a display with your whole team helps visualize the work-in-progress. At its simplest embodiment, you can share a to-do list with three columns: To-do, Doing, and Done. Everyone can see what's in the team's task queue if this list is shared using software or a whiteboard. You can also use a kanban board to post new, unclaimed tasks in the To-do column. When someone needs work, they pull a task by claiming it and moving it to the Doing column. Everyone can see who's doing what, and there's no time wasted asking, "What's left for me to do?"

Jidoka

This term (pronounced jid-oak-ah) means "automation with a human touch" and is another pillar of lean thinking. You can benefit from the speed of machines and computers while applying some human intelligence and oversight. This hybrid approach allows complex processes to be completed the correct way.

Too much automation can add complexity and reduce flexibility. You need to find the right combination of time-saving tools and smart people who use those tools.

After some setbacks at Tesla's first car factory, Elon Musk admitted, "Yes, excessive automation at Tesla was a mistake. To be precise, my mistake. Humans are underrated."[8]

A useful tool in implementing Jidoka is *andon,* which comes from the Japanese word meaning "light" or "lantern." A team member can alert the team when they see a problem. On a factory floor, the alert is triggered by pulling an "andon cord" that sounds an alarm. This pauses the normal pace so that the team member can receive help to resolve the problem. The person pulling the andon cord is not vilified for "slowing things down." Instead, they are respected for their willingness to make things right. A brief pause to fix a problem prevents customer complaints and avoids wasted time spent on rework. It also avoids problems down the line in subsequent processes. In some cases, issuing an alert can prevent a serious accident or life-threatening defect.

Pulling the andon cord is similar to calling a time-out. Surgical teams take a time-out before surgery to ensure they perform the right procedure on the right patient on the right side of the body.[9]

Sports teams take a time-out to review the upcoming play or make a change in strategy. In a similar way, allow your team members to take a brief time-out to make corrections to your semi-automated processes.

Poka yoke

This Japanese term (pronounced po-kah yo-kay) means "mistake-proofing," or preventing inadvertent errors by making it difficult or impossible to run a process the wrong way. Some examples of this technique in practice:

- A plug that fits into the outlet only the proper way.
- A tool with a purple stripe on its handle that is stored in the purple storage drawer. Or a cable with a green end that fits into the green port on the computer.
- A washing machine that won't run unless the door is closed.
- Text editing software that adds colorful underlines to your misspellings and grammar mistakes.
- A lawnmower that won't run unless you hold a bar near the handle.
- A vehicle that won't operate unless you've buckled your seatbelt.

Photocopier manufacturers use colored, numbered levers to indicate what to move (and in what sequence) to resolve a paper jam. The How-to Guide for the copier is part of the machine itself.

It takes time to design and install a poka yoke, but once it's in place, it's much easier to complete the task without making a mistake. Show respect for people by investing the time needed to protect them from preventable errors.

Genchi Genbutsu

This term (pronounced gen-chee gen-boo-tsoo) means "real location, real thing." This idea is also referred to as "go and see for yourself" or "get your boots on."[10]

The principle is that you should get out into the field and understand a problem first-hand. Observe what's happening to get improvement ideas based on what you've seen, not just what you've heard.

How to improve: look for uneven documentation coverage

Find processes that have no documentation or are missing explanations. Every repeating process should have a How-to Guide that explains how to run that process. Choose the level of detail based on how complex the process is, how critical the process is, and how costly an error would be.

How to improve: prepare for disruptions

Your processes need to be resilient. You need to anticipate and plan for disruptions. Risks are all around us, and they can't all be eliminated. Prepare for scenarios to make sure your organization survives.

You need to be ready for a variety of disruptions:

- Mistakes: errors, omissions, security lapses, regulatory infractions
- Staffing: departures, disputes
- Misconduct: cheating, embezzlement, harassment, theft, vandalism, cyberattacks, threats
- Accidents
- Regulatory changes: taxes, tariffs, restrictions, fees, requirements
- Natural disasters and bad weather
- Health emergencies
- Fire and smoke
- Media: unexpected coverage, viral content
- Equipment breakdowns
- Product liabilities, defects, and recalls
- Transportation delays: shutdowns, cancellations, blockages
- Service outages: Internet, electricity, water, gas, phone, HVAC
- Supply chain shortages
- Lawsuits

- Actions by other companies: mergers, takeovers, competition, new technology, new products, price changes
- Actions by individuals: protests, boycotts, strikes, lost items, uncooperativeness, slowdowns
- Macroeconomic factors: interest rates, exchange rates, inflation, wage rates

You can minimize the impact of these unexpected events by planning ahead. For some of these disruptions, especially ones originating inside your organization, you can take steps to prevent them from occurring.

As an example, a friend of mine left his work laptop in his parked car. Someone broke into his car and stole the laptop. The problem was that the laptop contained a file with Social Security numbers and personal data for some of his co-workers. The data file was left over from a project he was working on. Let's apply the "people problem or process problem?" diagnostic. At first glance, this is a people problem since my friend chose to leave his laptop in his car. But I think my friend was not 100% at fault since there were some process problems, too. How was it possible for him to download the personal information onto his laptop in the first place? Had he been trained never to keep that information on his laptop? Had he been told never to leave his work laptop in a car? Why was the laptop not encrypted? It's safe to assume that at some point, even with reasonable precautions, an employee's laptop will be stolen or lost. If the organization has not prepared for that disruption, then that points to a process problem. Asking some simple questions and creating some basic processes can help prepare for a stolen laptop scenario.

How to improve: prioritize

Now that you have developed a Process Library, you can refine your processes by finding the ones that have the biggest impact on achieving your business goals.

How to prioritize based on risk

We've looked at preparing for disruptions, but you can also prioritize your response to potential problems using a finer-grained approach to assess risk. You can decide what processes you'll need to improve to minimize the damage.

For each type of disruption, estimate the likelihood and the severity.

- To assess the likelihood of the disruption, ask these questions:
  - How often does this occur in our business? In our industry? In similar businesses?
  - Is this linked to other events? If so, how often do those other events occur?
- To assess the severity of the disruption, ask these questions:
  - What is the maximum potential loss?
  - What is the most likely amount of loss?
  - What is the expected recovery time from the disruption?
  - Who does this affect, both inside and outside our organization?
  - Do we have a backup for anything that we lose?
  - Is this a never event (something that should never occur under any circumstance)?

Start with the most likely disruptions or the ones resulting in the greatest loss, or combine those two measures and prioritize processes with the largest "risk score."

Create or improve processes that help prevent and mitigate the damage from the disruption. You should ask the following questions:

- Do we have a process in place for each type of disruption?
- Are we applying the best methods in our industry?
- How do others solve this?
- What has worked for us in the past? What has not worked?
- Is it possible to insure against this disruption? If so, what level of insurance is appropriate? Or can we self-insure? Or partially self-insure by choosing a larger deductible?
- What is our Plan B if a disruption occurs?

- What should we do immediately, as a first step?

How to prioritize by impact, cost, and frequency

To triage process improvement opportunities, consider both impact and cost. To assess impact, estimate the benefits that an improved process would provide. The benefit could be higher profit, lower cost, or greater customer retention. To assess cost, estimate the time and cost required to improve the process. Now you can sort opportunities into four categories:

- High impact + low cost. Pursue these first.
- High impact + high cost. Look for ways to lower the cost of improving these processes.
- Low impact + low cost. Rank these further, and consider the lowest-cost ones first.
- Low impact + high cost. Save these for last. Or delay pursuing these until the cost is justified.

Also, consider the frequency of a process. Which processes are performed the most often? This can affect your impact assessment.

After assessing impact, cost, and frequency, add labels to the priority processes in your Process Library to preserve the results of your analysis.

How to prioritize by function and focus

Your Process Matrix provides a view of your processes by functional areas (in columns) and focus areas (in rows). Look at the intersection of each functional area and focus area to see if some need more attention. For example, at the intersection of your Sales column and Strategy row, you discover that you're lacking long-range, intentional goals for Sales Strategy. In response, you can prioritize the development of a process such as "How to set sales goals and objectives."

How to improve: use 1-to-1 weekly meetings

We explored 1-to-1 meetings in Chapter 11. Use these meetings as part of your ongoing process improvement. A supervisor can meet 1-to-1 with a direct report to review concerns and discuss process improvements. Use 1-

to-1 meetings to find and resolve problems before they get too big. Set goals for creating new How-to Guides where needed, refining existing How-to Guides, or identifying the flow of a process.

How to improve: develop metrics

Think about measurements that will help you understand how well a process is performing. These metrics should be easy to gather and record. Here are some examples:

- How well does the output match the standard?
- How often do we encounter an error or problem with the process?
- How long does this process take to complete?
- How satisfied are our customers with this process? Also, consider customers inside your organization.

As you consider diagnostics that will help visualize changes and improvements, don't become so enamored by capturing the metrics that you neglect improvement. Don't be all talk and no action.

How to improve: diagram your processes

A diagram can show how processes depend on each other or how the steps flow in one process.

Process flow diagram

A simple process flow diagram uses a rectangle for each step and arrows to point to the next steps. Decision steps are diamonds that branch to multiple next steps based on what is decided. Figure 13-1 shows an example flowchart for how to troubleshoot a lamp.

Figure 13-1. Process Flowchart. Create a flowchart to help visualize the sequence and decisions within a process.

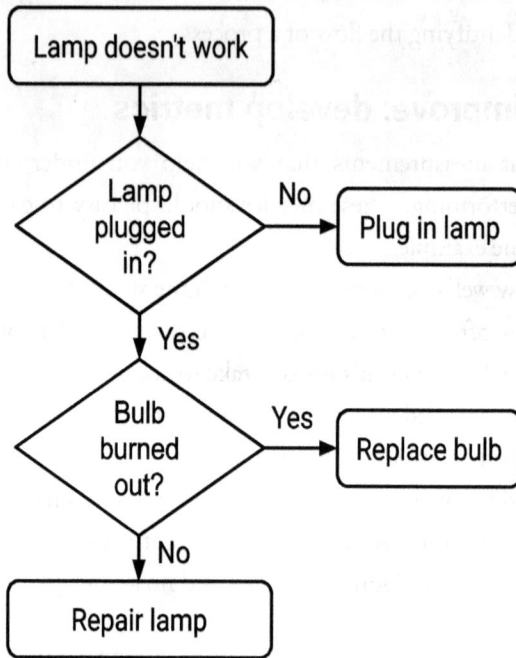

To reveal potential bottlenecks and wasted effort, label each process step with its duration. The diagram shows dependencies, so you know how a change in one step will affect the other steps downstream.

Swimlane chart

To make a "swimlane" flowchart, create a column for each role or department involved in a process. List the process steps in the proper column, from start to finish, moving down the page. Add arrows showing the flow between the process steps. If there are too many roles or handoffs, simplify the process. Figure 13-2 shows an example swimlane chart.

Figure 13-2. Swimlane Chart. Create a swimlane chart to see both the flow and the assigned roles.

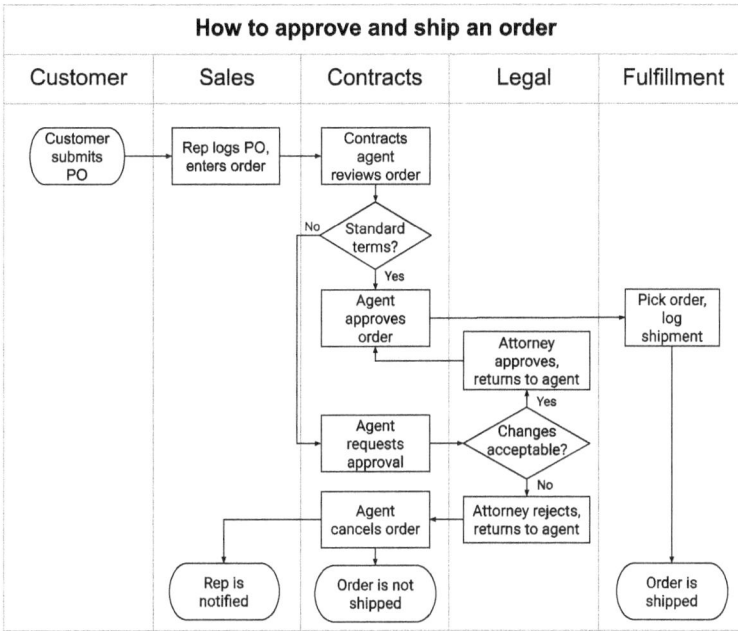

SIPOC chart

This high-level chart summarizes a process by listing the suppliers, inputs, process steps, outputs, and customers ("SIPOC" for short) in five separate columns. Use this chart to find ways to streamline the process and create a faster flow, beginning to end.

Value stream mapping

You can further refine your process diagram with a value stream map. Draw a "current state" flowchart that shows each step in the progression from raw inputs to the final step, where your customer benefits from your product or service. Attach a timeline and duration to each step of the process.

Identify the steps that directly benefit the customer. In a manufacturing setting, true value is only created when the product changes and progresses toward completion. In other words, something is being done that the customer is willing to pay for. In a services business, workers add value when they take actions that bring the customer closer to a desired result, which the customer is willing to pay for.

Calculate the total elapsed time for the entire process, start-to-finish. Also, calculate the sum of just the valued-added time. The difference between the total elapsed time and the value-added time represents waste that you can target for removal.

Look for the weakest links in the value stream. Where do people wait for inputs from a previous step? Do raw materials accumulate while waiting to be processed? Do piles of unfinished work accumulate? Does finished work accumulate, waiting to be delivered? Reduce inventory and work-in-progress to serve your customers faster and accelerate cash flow.

A word of caution about diagrams: not all processes need them. If a process has just a few steps, or if a process proceeds from start to finish with no decisions, then a diagram would only serve to convert a list of steps into a collection of rectangles, which does not add much insight.

How to improve: automate your processes

Are you manually inspecting or approving something that should be done right the first time instead? If so, help people check their own output as they work. You can also automate the verification process.

As you identify and refine your processes, label the ones that are candidates for automation. Also, label your processes that are already automated. For example, here are labels that could track automation possibilities for a process:

- automation: candidate
- automation: to-do-hi-priority
- automation: to-do-med-priority
- automation: in-progress
- automation: partial
- automation: full

Let's look at some specific ways to automate your processes.

Minimize email, spreadsheets, and paper

Email, spreadsheets, and paper documents breed errors since those tools lack the consistency that structured software provides. As you identify processes that rely on paper, email, and spreadsheets, find standardization opportunities. You can decide whether using more specialized software would be worth it.

If you use any of these to complete ongoing tasks, there may be automation opportunities.

- Paper. This includes forms and reports. Look for ways to receive and route these items without needing to handle a paper copy. Convert paper forms to online versions and scan existing paper documents into a shared digital repository.

- Spreadsheets. These are useful for tracking, planning, and budgeting but try to move these functions into your core business applications. Make sure you're using all the features of your current software to minimize the use of spreadsheets. If you use spreadsheets to track essential parts of your business, such as processes, finances, and deadlines, you may want to upgrade to an app that handles that tracking in a more consistent way.

- Email. This includes notifications, reminders, or requests for approval that are sent manually. Look for ways to automate reminders and requests for information.

Add intelligence to forms

Even if your forms are online, make sure you are taking full advantage of features to save time for the person submitting a form and for the person receiving a form.

- Calculations. Can you perform calculations as part of the form's logic, saving the recipient from having to crunch the numbers?
- Error-checking. Can you validate form entries before submission? For example, validate that phone numbers, email addresses, and mailing addresses are in the correct format.

- Required fields. Have you required that all necessary fields be completed?
- Routing. Can you automatically send the form results to the proper person without an intermediary? Can you route submissions directly to a collaboration app or shared database?
- Look-ups. Can you provide a pick list of the possible answers to a question on the form?
- Conditional sections. Can you ask a question and then hide or display sections of the form based on the answer? Remove visual clutter and make the form easier to fill out.

Use automation tools

In a factory setting, automation often involves machines and robots. Software robots can also be used in an office setting. Process automation software can save time when doing repetitive tasks. Automate common tasks using a visual workflow editor or by writing scripts.

Pick an automation or artificial intelligence (AI) tool and try automating just one of your process. Build on that success, or learn from the challenges you encounter. Once you have automated a process, find more processes to automate, starting with the simplest ones.

Add a label to each automated process in your Process Library indicating which automation tool you used. Filter your processes by the tool used and find similar processes that could be automated. Also, if you need to switch automation tools in the future, you will have an instant inventory of the affected processes.

Look for repetition

Look for tasks that are repeated with minor variations. Use a program or script to combine the variable information with a template, creating a customized version with minimal effort. For example,

- Instead of calling patients to confirm their appointments, a dentist can use a service that makes automated reminder calls or sends reminder text messages.

- Instead of manually creating summary reports, write a program to collect results and create the summary.
- Instead of making the boarding announcement at the airport, the gate attendant can press a button to play a pre-recorded message that includes the flight number, destination, and boarding instructions.

How to improve: develop a culture of process thinking

As you begin to view your business as a collection of interconnected systems, enlist other team members to build on this foundation. Add process-related activities into the rhythm of your daily and weekly routines. Be intentional with your process improvements. Make sure you have some strategy-related processes for each functional area. Set aside time (at least annually) to think deeply about pathways and journeys.

- How do we help people discover us and become customers?
- How do we help our customers move from brand new to raving fans?
- How do we move from informal processes to refined, documented, and automated processes?
- How do we move from an idea to a viable product?
- How do we move from a good product to a great product?
- How do we help our team members become experts?

Putting people first creates a strong foundation for building the rest of your processes. When building a culture of process thinking, make sure you have covered a core set of people-focused processes:

- How do we train our people?
- How do we encourage, recognize, and reward our people?
- How do we evaluate and guide our people?
- How do we work together to reach a shared objective?

How to improve: let frustrations become processes opportunities

In other words, fix what bugs you. If a process irritates or frustrates you, channel your negative energy and work to change the process.

A friend of mine serves on the Board of Directors for a small manufacturing company. Recently he learned that $40,000 had been paid to another organization without any clear record of what the money was spent on. Sloppiness like that could open the door to other problems. He had to piece together what happened based on verbal descriptions. He was frustrated. Actually, *irate* is the better word.

Was this a people problem (where someone wasn't following a written process) or a process problem (where there was no clear process)? It was a process problem. There was no written process about how to buy something.

Here's a simple How-to Guide that could have prevented the problem:

How to make a purchase (simple version)

1. Get written Board approval if over $10,000. Every time, no exceptions.
2. Get a detailed receipt. Every time, no exceptions.

Here's a more detailed version of this How-to Guide that could have organized all the purchase receipts.

How to make a purchase (more detailed version)

1. Get approval as follows for different expense amounts:
    -   If over $10,000, get approval in writing from the Board.
    -   If over $1,000, get approval from the General Manager.
    -   If under $1,000, no approval is needed for a budgeted expense. A non-budgeted expense over $100 needs approval from the General Manager.
2. Pay the vendor
    -   If over $1,000, the General Manager uses our bank's bill-pay service.
    -   If under $1,000, use the company debit card.

3. Get documentation of the purchase. Obtain a receipt for each purchase that includes the following:
    ◦ Seller's name and contact info
    ◦ Description of items purchased
    ◦ Amount paid for each item and the total amount
4. File the receipt
    ◦ Download, scan, or photograph the receipt
    ◦ Store the receipt on the shared drive in this folder: Dropbox / Accounting / Receipts / {current month's folder}
    ◦ Name the file as follows:
        ▪ YYYY-MM-DD + Recipient + Purchase Description
        ▪ example: 202x-07-18 Copies-N-More Training Workbooks.pdf

The effectiveness of this process depends on people using it correctly. But even if they don't, at least you've converted a process problem into a people problem. Solve people problems with better hiring, training, and incentives.

Even small frustrations can reveal process problems. I received a call from my dentist's office canceling an upcoming appointment since the dentist's schedule had changed. It was helpful that they called the patients who were affected by the change in schedule. But after receiving the phone call, I later received a text message reminding me of the appointment that had already been canceled. Their process didn't include canceling the automated reminder message.

Another example of a small glitch revealing a process opportunity is a church sign that still says "Happy Mother's Day" two weeks after the holiday. Not following a process to change their sign, means they've missed an opportunity to tell their community about something new. They may also have indicated that they're careless with details, which is not good for a church. In contrast, if you visit a Costco store the day after Christmas, that holiday is a memory and they're displaying workout gear and vitamins. They waste no opportunity.

How to improve: ask improvement questions

Ask questions about your current processes to find top improvement opportunities, then label and prioritize. For example, if you have a high-margin service you want to refine and grow, ask which processes relate to that service. Label those processes and apply a filter to see everything that needs to be addressed to grow that service.

Here are some questions to find improvement ideas.

Accelerating Growth

- What processes are constraining our ability to scale up?
- What processes have the greatest difficulty with repeatability and consistency?
- What processes need to be changed, but "we've always done it this way?"
- What processes should be replicated or standardized across departments or team members?
- What processes do customers find the most frustrating, stressful, or annoying?
- What processes have the greatest effect on customer satisfaction?
- What processes need more scalability to replicate across more customers and generate more profit?
- What processes have the greatest effect on our company's reputation?
- What processes have the greatest effect on our business partners and vendors?
- What processes provide the most and least value for customers?

Streamlining Operations

- What processes need more accuracy and fewer errors?
- What processes need more visibility so we can see exactly how they work?
- What processes need better on-time performance?
- What processes need better predictability?

- What processes need to be completed more consistently?
- What processes do suppliers find the most frustrating, stressful, or annoying?
- What processes take the most time from our leaders and executives?
- What processes are the most frustrating, stressful, or annoying for the business owners?
- What processes work okay but need more refinement?
- What processes are unclear or confusing?
- What processes are easiest to improve?

Optimizing Coverage

- What processes should exist but don't? Where are the process gaps?
- What processes could be combined?
- What processes should be separated, disaggregated, or made more granular?
- What processes have documentation that is too sparse? Or not clear enough?
- What processes would benefit from a flowchart, checklist, diagram, table, or chart?

Thinking Lean

- What processes have too many steps and need streamlining?
- What processes generate errors?
- What processes duplicate efforts by different people?
- What processes most often have rework or re-dos?
- What processes are using "demand push" when they should be using "demand pull?"
- What processes need to be measured for their effectiveness?
- What processes need their cycle time measured?
- What processes need a faster cycle time?
- What processes need a faster recovery or reset time?

- What processes have the most waste?
- What processes could reduce excess inventory?
- What processes have wasted motion or effort?
- What processes have waiting times that are too long?

Mitigating Risk

- What processes expose us to the greatest risk of financial loss?
- What processes are most fragile or easily disrupted?
- What processes have a single point of failure?
- What processes need more compliance and verification?
- What processes need more redundancy, backup planning, or contingency planning?
- What processes need more visibility to understand the risks?
- What processes need more security and mitigation of vulnerabilities?
- What processes are most affected by someone leaving our organization?
- What processes have the most revenue risk, and how can that risk be mitigated?
- What processes have the most supply chain risk, and how can that risk be mitigated?

Leveraging Technology

- What processes could be streamlined by adding technology?
- What processes have the greatest potential for automation?
- What processes are underutilizing existing technology?
- What processes use different but similar technologies when they should use the same technology?
- What processes need more automation?
- What processes need to generate more data for better decision-making?

Supporting People

- What processes do team members find the most frustrating, stressful, or annoying?
- What processes need more training or better training?
- What processes are the most difficult for new team members to learn?
- What processes need more accountability?
- What processes need more load balancing across team members?
- What processes should be assigned to a different role?
- What processes have the greatest effect on team member satisfaction?
- What processes are currently in-house but could be performed better by a contractor?
- What processes are currently external (outsourced) but should be brought in-house?
- What processes need more delineation, clearer roles, and less fuzzy boundaries?
- What processes are too difficult for team members to follow?

Strengthening Finances

- What processes are the most expensive, and how can we reduce the cost?
- What processes are the least expensive, and what can we learn from these?
- What processes have the greatest revenue impact, and how can we increase revenue?
- What processes have the greatest effect on profit margin, and how can we improve them?
- What processes have the greatest effect on revenue consistency?
- What processes have the greatest effect on our business valuation?
- What processes could make the business more valuable or franchisable?

How to improve: don't stagnate with analysis

Value is only created when your product is being built, or your service is being provided. Everything else is waste. Be careful not to overanalyze what you are doing instead of actually doing it better.

Shigeo Shingo was a Japanese industrial engineer and an expert on the Toyota Production System. Ken Snyder, a Senior Lecturer at Utah State University, said this about Shingo:

> "He spent ten years studying statistical quality control, a lot of Deming's work and things like that. He said, 'I got enamored by it. I loved it.' And then, after about ten years he gradually began to realize it was a waste. He called it his 'lost ten years.' Why did he call it a waste? Because he was focusing on measuring and controlling defects instead of eliminating them."[11]

Set goals and track how well you're doing, but don't let the analysis get in the way of actually making the improvements.

Checklist for improving your processes

- [ ] Refine your How-to Guides as you use them. Make gradual progress. Don't try to improve everything at once.
- [ ] Experiment. "Fail fast" and try an alternate improvement method if one doesn't work.
- [ ] Embrace lean thinking and look for waste.
- [ ] Identify potential business disruptions and create How-to Guides for handling them.
- [ ] Respect people. Reward and celebrate improvement.
- [ ] Meet with your direct reports regularly to address questions and concerns.
- [ ] Develop a culture where it's expected that everyone helps improve how things work.
- [ ] For critical or slow processes, create a flow diagram and look for ways to automate or simplify.
- [ ] Collect frustrations and recast them as process improvement opportunities.

☐ Capture errors and questions for each process to improve reliability and clarity.

☐ Keep moving. Don't get sucked into "analysis paralysis."

Chapter 14

How to Improve Your Processes by Learning From Others

Identify	Describe	Use	Improve
Chapter 4. Identify Your **Functional Areas**		Chapter 10. Use Your Processes in **Day-to-Day Work**	Chapter 13. **Improve** Your Processes
Chapter 5. Identify Your **Roles**	Chapter 8. Describe Your Processes With **Attributes**	Chapter 11. Use Your Processes With **Your Team**	Chapter 14. Improve Your Processes by **Learning from Others**
Chapter 6. Identify Your **Processes**	Chapter 9. Describe Your Processes Using **How-To Guides**	Chapter 12. Use Your Processes With **Business Frameworks**	Chapter 15. Improve Your Processes Using **External Resources**
Chapter 7. Identify **Gaps and Opportunities**			

Think of companies that started small but grew to prominence: Toyota, Microsoft, McDonald's, Starbucks, and Amazon. All of these companies pay close attention to their processes. There is "a way we do things here" that is learned, taught, and improved.

Let's see what we can learn from some stories of process success.

Consider Nick Saban

Nick Saban, the U.S. college football coach, has won more NCAA football championships than anyone else. His not-so-secret secret? Something he calls "The Process." Coach Saban explains, "The process, to me, is just the definition of the things you have to do to accomplish the goals that you have."[1]

Colin Peek played for Georgia Tech before transferring to the University of Alabama under Coach Saban. Colin had this to say about the difference between the two football programs:

> "Programs talk about what they want to do and how they want to do it, but Coach Saban makes sure everything is written down. It's something you can visualize. They didn't have that at my old school [Georgia Tech]. They talked about things, but it wasn't reiterated like that."[2]

Under Coach Saban, things weren't just talked about; they were written down. Our memories aren't that great. If it's written down, we can do lots of useful things that we can't do if it's just talked about: we can read it, share it, edit it, memorize it, summarize it, teach it, print it, diagram it, post it, and comment on it.

Kirby Smart, an assistant coach under Saban, had this to say about Saban's methods, "Number one thing I took away is he spends more time on how to do it than any other head coach in the country. Just obsessed with the details, [he] concerns himself with how to do it rather than just what to do."[3]

Coach Saban's former assistants have absorbed this "process thinking." Jimbo Fisher, one of Saban's former assistant coaches, explained, "When [our kicker] misses in practice, I say 'Trust the process; go back to fundamentals. Play the next play. Ignore the scoreboard.'"[4]

Ideas from Nick Saban
- Define each player's role and clarify that role's assignments and expectations.
- Help each player do their job by providing instruction and encouragement.
- Reinforce accountability with a routine of analyzing completed work (i.e., the weekly game film) and looking for ways to improve.

Consider Justin Langer

Great coaches in all sports across every continent, focus on processes. Justin Langer is a former professional cricket player and the coach of Australia's national team. He offers this insight:

> "I knew, as a batsman, if I got balanced in my stance, and I saw the ball out of the bowler's hand, everything would be okay. So that's process. So as a coach, I'm very much about 'just get the preparation right; get the processes right.' The great players just concentrate every single ball. Every great Australian player has been great at the process of the next ball. That's all. It's the easiest way to get 100. It's the easiest way for us to get 320."[5]

Scoring 100 runs in one inning is a "century," a notable achievement for a single batsman. Scoring 320 runs as a team usually results in victory.

Ideas from Justin Langer
- Work to understand and visualize each part of a process.
- Prepare and train for high-pressure moments. Improve your ability to concentrate on the task at hand.

Consider McKinsey & Co.

The consultants at this international consulting firm are elite, smart, and able to handle a wide range of business problems. They're the "Navy Seals" of business. They jump into companies, assess the situation, identify needs and gaps, and develop solutions based on their experience and industry knowledge. They work side-by-side with leaders at the company to achieve strategic objectives.

But this ability relies on a set of tried-and-true processes:

- How to recruit new consultants. McKinsey presents realistic case studies during an interview and expects an interviewee to contribute some immediate, intelligent insights about the problem.

- How to preserve prior work and discoveries. McKinsey maintains a searchable database of prior work so that consultants can build on solutions developed in other offices worldwide.

- How to create and use "frameworks" to solve business problems. McKinsey consultants document specific approaches for solving certain types of business problems. When working on client engagement, consultants can adapt a framework to a client's particular needs. Classic McKinsey frameworks include the following:

  ○ The Portfolio of Initiatives. This describes how to "develop a strategy in a more fluid, less predictable environment."[6]

  ○ Customer Decision Journey. This describes how to optimize your customers' path from initial consideration to becoming part of a "loyalty loop."[7]

  ○ The Three Horizons of Growth. This describes "how to manage for current performance while maximizing future opportunities for growth."[8]

- How to train new team members. McKinsey provides an intensive mini-MBA course for consultants with technical backgrounds who need more business knowledge.

Ideas from McKinsey & Co.

- Preserve valuable knowledge from completed projects.
- Document successful approaches that will apply to future situations.
- Standardize the way prospective employees are evaluated.

Consider Walters & Wolf

This California construction company manufactures and installs windows. It sounds simple, but it takes many steps to ensure that a window in a commercial building is installed properly. Windows should keep people inside, keep the harsh weather outside, and look good while doing it. Windows must be safe, energy-efficient, installed correctly, and maintained properly. Walters & Wolf carefully documents the step-by-step process for each type of product and service they provide. For example, Walters & Wolf has a process for "How to fabricate and install a segmented wall of windows."[9] This process has the following steps:

1. Jumpstart. Get the project kicked off with everyone in sync.
2. Family setup. Copy the files and templates for a new project.
3. Drafting. Draw and revise all the windows needed for the project.
4. Takeoffs. Take measurements from the drawings for costing and fabrication.
5. Fabs. Fabricate the parts and pieces that are needed.
6. Shop. Assemble the windows from the various parts.
7. Field. Install the windows at the customer site.

Each of these seven areas is further subdivided into sub-processes with detailed instructions about how to perform each step. Every day the company publishes a new video explaining some aspect of a process. Not only do they have processes for installing windows, they also have processes for how to improve their processes. It's a virtuous cycle that helps them get better and makes their customers happier.

Ideas from Walters & Wolf

- Sub-divide lengthy or complex processes into steps or smaller processes.
- Create a startup process that gets files and materials organized before work begins.
- Commit to a routine of publishing process improvement techniques.

To see more benefits of clearly defined processes, let's look at two industries where people's lives depend on proper processes: aviation and healthcare.

Consider the Boeing 777

Most people who fly on a plane take for granted that it will get there safely. For others who fear flying, it can be an unsettling experience. We can all be confident that a combination of rules, policies, and training work together to create the safest possible flight.

One key component of safe air travel is the checklist.

Despite pilots and flight officers having thousands of hours of experience, they use checklists on every flight.[10] Consider the checklists that must be a part of every flight on a Boeing 777 jet:

- Before Start checklist
- Start checklist
- Before Taxi checklist
- Before Takeoff checklist
- After Takeoff checklist
- *Most of the flying time occurs here, hopefully without incident.*
- Descent checklist
- Approach checklist
- Landing checklist
- Shutdown checklist
- Secure checklist

Maybe you're thinking, "That's too many checklists. It's unreasonable. Pilots are trained professionals. They know what to do! Don't micromanage them!"

As passengers in that aluminum tube jetting through the air, we do not consider the checklists unreasonable. We understand that when operating such a sophisticated collection of systems like a Boeing 777 airliner, it's difficult to remember how to do everything correctly every time. And our lives are at stake.

Also, there are rare, unplanned situations that can occur. For those critical and life-threatening events, there are dozens of "Non-normal checklists" (NNCs), such as the following:

- Engine Fire
- Engine Failure
- Pilot Incapacitation
- Window Damage
- Fuel Leak

These checklists contain the best ways to resolve each problem based on the plane's design. The pilot's skills are needed to run through each checklist, but speed and clarity are vital when your plane's engine is on fire.

Like a Boeing 777, your business is a collection of interdependent systems. You have multiple people with multiple skills using different technologies to meet diverse customer needs using many different processes. Over time, you've refined this collection of systems to deliver results.

The airline industry is helpful to study since they do an incredible job of keeping travel safe. Every year the industry learns how to make air travel safer. Each accident is analyzed, and procedures are changed to prevent future problems. Even as air travel has surged in popularity, the number of fatal accidents per year has declined.

My friend Douglas, who served in the military as a helicopter pilot and as an accident investigator, made this observation about processes, "When we analyzed crashes, over half the time, a process was not followed correctly. Having the methodologies and tools to implement a proactive process for spotting problems is critical to creating a culture of safety. The key to this process is time—the sooner a problem is identified the more likely it is that a dangerous situation can be averted."

Ideas from the Boeing 777 and the airline industry
- Create checklists to improve safety and consistency.
- Analyze failures to find ways to minimize chances of a recurrence.

Consider Dr. Provonost

Healthcare, another life-or-death industry, also provides useful process stories.

In 2001, a central line infection was a routine complication of a patient's stay in an intensive care unit. A central line is an intravenous catheter that extends into the body near the heart. Four percent of central lines would become infected after ten days. Between five and twenty-eight percent of those infections would lead to death. With 80,000 central line infections occurring each year, that's 4,000 to 22,400 deaths per year.

Do we accept these deaths as the "cost of doing business" and move forward with our lives? Peter Provonost, a physician and professor at the Johns Hopkins School of Medicine, decided not to accept the status quo. He developed a simple checklist that he thought would prevent central line infections. He based the checklist on five well-known steps that not everyone followed.

Here is Dr. Provonost's checklist to reduce catheter-related bloodstream infections:

1. Wash your hands before inserting a central venous catheter (CVC)
2. Clean the patient's skin with chlorhexidine
3. Use of full-barrier precautions during CVC insertion. (e.g., cap, mask, sterile gown, sterile gloves, and large sterile drape)
4. Avoid the femoral site
5. Remove unnecessary CVCs; evaluate daily the need for the continued use of the CVC

To make this even easier to remember, we could summarize this in 15 words:

1. Wash your hands
2. Clean with chlorhexidine
3. Use full-barrier precautions
4. Avoid femoral site
5. Re-evaluate CVCs daily

Although I'm not a doctor, some of these seem obvious. Do I really need to be told to wash my hands? Seriously? Do we really need a checklist for these? Aren't these totally obvious, based on common sense?

If we insist that doctors follow this checklist, wouldn't we be insulting the intelligence of these highly-educated, highly-trained professionals?

Well, what's worse: a possible insult or thousands of dead patients?

Another concern might be, "Do we make doctors less innovative if we insist they use a checklist?" No more than insisting that a veteran pilot land a Boeing 777 using a checklist. Instead of stifling innovation, a checklist frees a doctor from overthinking the simple stuff. The doctor can focus on more complex tasks such as improving safety, diagnosing cases, collaborating with colleagues, and solving problems. If a simple checklist like the one Dr. Provonost created can save lives, we should use it, not fight it.

But did Dr. Provonost's checklist actually help?

Dr. Provonost's checklist began to get widespread acceptance. From 2001 to 2009, the infection rate in intensive care units dropped from 48,000 to 19,000. That's thousands of lives saved.[11]

Atul Gawande has much more to say about the value of checklists in his book *The Checklist Manifesto: How to Get Things Right*. Gawande asserts that we should look for patterns in our failures and then use checklists as simple tools to overcome failure.[12]

Wise leaders can ask: How can we be more like an airline in terms of safety and consistency? What can we learn from the safest hospitals and physicians about how to care for our customers?

Ideas from Dr. Provonost
- Ignore the naysayers who want to maintain the status quo.
- Distill checklists down to the essential items.
- Use checklists even with senior leadership.

Stories of Process Failure

Now let's turn our attention to some stories about poor processes. We explore these failures not because of *schadenfreude*—taking joy in others' suffering—but because every time we see a failure, we can find an opportunity to improve.

By examining both large and small failures, we can discover root causes. It's often the small failures, when ignored, that lead to huge failures.

Some failures are unavoidable. Some things are acts of God or a combination of adverse events that could not have been foreseen. A process may not prevent those events, but could help minimize the loss or damage. Having a process can also speed up recovery.

Bad weather may disrupt our business, but having a process allows us to minimize downtime.

Hackers may attack our company's information systems, but having a process can protect vital data and reduce the damage these cybercriminals cause.

Customers may not follow the directions for using our product or service, but having a process allows us to help them when they have a problem.

Process failure at a non-profit

I was invited to attend a seminar on a campus with several buildings. I accepted the invitation and noted of the date, time, and campus address.

A day before the event, I received a helpful reminder email from the host, but the email didn't include the room number or how to find the event's location. Upon arriving, I asked someone at the reception desk if they knew about the event. They did not, so I headed toward where I thought the event was. As I wandered the halls, I encountered more people looking for the same event. None of us knew where to go. If there were 100 invitees, how many minutes were wasted by people wandering around trying to find the right room?

Ideas from this non-profit

- Use an invitation template and reminder template.
- Anticipate the information your customer needs. For example, provide instructions for where to park, what entrance to use, and how to get to the meeting room.

Process failure at a doctor's office

When I went in for a routine doctor's visit, I checked in at the front desk and was asked for my driver's license and contact information. As part of my visit, they ran a blood test. I requested that a copy of the blood test results be sent to me for my files. "No problem, we will be glad to mail that," they replied. After waiting for the results for two weeks, I called to check on the status. They had sent my blood test results to my old home address from years ago.

I wasted time investigating the delay, and they wasted time and money having to re-send the test results. A simple solution would have been to verify my mailing address when I checked in.

Ideas from this doctor's office

- Ask customers if anything has changed in order to provide better service and discover new opportunities.
- Use a secure online portal for document delivery instead of postal mail, which can be misdelivered.

Process failures at a school

With hundreds of students, dozens of teachers, and thousands of personal interactions every day, schools are ripe for process problems.

Just looking at the area of communication, here are some examples of problems:

- Parents and students are not notified of changes to lesson plans or assignments. This ambiguity leads to confusion and time wasted getting clarification.
- Lesson plans or assignments are not released or published on time.
- Quizzes and assignments are not returned to students prior to a test. The students don't have the chance to learn from their past mistakes.
- Teachers don't collaborate or share when creating lesson plans, so a lot of work gets duplicated.

- Instructions for a substitute teacher are incomplete or missing. The students don't learn much from the sub.
- Teachers are surprised to learn about a meeting that's not on the calendar. This is frustrating since they were not expecting to work those extra hours.

Ideas from a school
- When expectations or assignments change, have a standard way of notifying all those affected.
- Document unpleasant surprises and frustrations, then apply the "People or Process?" framework to find root causes and solutions.

Process failures in my early career

In my first job out of college, I worked for a market research firm that focused on the natural gas industry. My boss tasked me with creating a directory of industrial natural gas consumers. To do this, we needed to call hundreds of businesses and factories to ask about their natural gas usage. We assembled a team of three surveyors who would make phone calls. They would interview natural gas buyers and record answers on forms that I designed.

To inspire the team and kick off the project, I called a meeting. I printed a page for each attendee with the word "QUALITY" in giant letters. I presented this to the surveyors with a dramatic flourish. I thought I could emphasize this one word and talk in generalities about quality. Then everyone would do a better job of getting the precise information we needed. It was a naïve approach.

Quality stems from the ability to meet a specified standard. Meeting that standard was not something that we could achieve by staring at the word QUALITY in ALL CAPS. Instead, I would have been better off using a process-driven approach. I should have focused on helping the surveyors master each step of the process. The resulting quality would have taken care of itself.

I failed to understand the best way to achieve the needed results. A better use of time would have been sharing ideas for defining and refining the survey process. We could have discussed the following:

- How to get the right person on the phone
- How to introduce yourself
- How to respond to the interviewee's questions or concerns
- How to conduct the interview. For example, use a script with branching options based on how the interviewee answers the questions.
- How to conclude the call
- How to record the data you collect

We also could have created a troubleshooting guide for challenges that would occur, such as the following:

- If you reach a wrong number, then do this.
- If you can't reach a knowledgeable person, then do this.

Despite my naïveté, we managed to complete the project and create a useful directory, but I didn't help the process as much as I could have.

Ideas from this early career project

- Clear instruction is more useful than incredible encouragement. Combine direction with motivation.
- Don't speak only in terms of platitudes and generalities; get specific.

Process failures at HealthIQ

I saw an ad for life insurance from a company called HealthIQ that intrigued me. They offered lower rates for people with healthy lifestyles, including runners, cyclists, swimmers, and vegans. I knew life insurance rates were lower for non-smokers, but I hadn't heard of anyone offering discounts using this particular health angle. Since I try to stay healthy, I thought I might qualify.

I took the bait and called them for a quote.

It started off well. The sales consultant answered all my questions, took my information, and helped me complete the application.

Then the problems began. When I had some additional questions, the consultant told me I needed to talk to someone else. When the application they sent me to sign had errors (which were not my fault), I was referred to another person. When I contacted that person, I got no response. I still got no response when I contacted them a second and third time. Only after I escalated this to my original sales contact was I able to get things resolved.

For a couple of weeks, I received emails referring to at least seven different people: Karina, Alexandra, Bryanna, Kevin, Ali, Sofia, and Terri. The documents I needed to sign came from a separate company. On top of that, I received emails from seven other generic healthiq.com addresses: insurance, concierge, applications, support, finalapprovals, mypolicy, and ceo.

Whew. It's like there was an explosion at the email server, and "from:" addresses got splattered everywhere.

After my insurance policy was finally issued, I received a survey from "ceo@healthiq.com" to rate my satisfaction. Even that was messed up. The survey asked about my experience with Ryan, my case manager. I never interacted with anyone named Ryan.

In a spirit of helpfulness (okay, combined with frustration), I replied to the CEO's email and described my less-than-ideal experience. I assumed the survey was sent automatically, so I expressed doubt that the CEO would even see my response.

But the CEO did respond by email. He wrote, "I am the CEO of Health IQ. I wanted to let you know I've read this. I really appreciate the feedback and will likely make some changes based upon your detailed notes. I'll reach back out in a week or two with some concrete ideas / or have a call to understand the issues in more detail."

Sadly (or predictably?), the CEO did not fulfill his promise to "reach back out in a week or two." I never heard from him again. Perhaps they lack a process for customer follow-up.

I suspect that this customer service debacle resulted from a rapidly growing company that launched an aggressive marketing campaign to get new customers but didn't bother to consider the start-to-finish process that a new customer experiences.

A basic step-by-step description of a new customer's journey would have revealed where they had major problems. Their process could have been simplified to allow me to interact with just two people: the sales rep and the insurance agent. Even simpler, what if I just spoke with one person who could handle everything?

Ideas from HealthIQ

- Visualize or experience the customer's journey and remove delays and annoyances.
- Keep your promises, or at least don't make insincere commitments.

Process failures on Fine Air Flight 101

Failures in the airline industry can illustrate problems caused by flawed processes. An airplane is a complex collection of systems: avionics, fuel, electrical, propulsion, and crew. Planes need a high level of human skill to operate. Improper operation or communication between these systems can have fatal consequences.

One example is the case of Fine Air Flight 101 on August 7, 1997.

Aeromar, a freight company, chartered a DC-8 cargo plane from Fine Air to transport denim fabric from Miami to the Dominican Republic. Aeromar employees at the airport would load and unload the cargo, but Fine Air pilots would fly the plane.

At 2:55 a.m., an Aeromar employee prepared to load the cargo by faxing a description of the cargo pallets to the Fine Air flight follower, who was responsible for preparing the loading plan. The flight follower created and sent the loading plan to Aeromar. The plan showed how to load the pallets to achieve the proper weight balance.

Meanwhile, the original plane scheduled to carry the cargo got delayed and had not arrived in Miami. To avoid additional delays, Fine Air decided to substitute a similar plane that was heavier than the original plane chosen for the flight.

Because of the heavier plane, the Fine Air flight follower noted that Aeromar should remove 1,000 pounds of cargo. At 7:00 a.m., the flight follower called a security guard at the cargo hanger and told him about the need to reduce weight. The security guard called the Aeromar Operations Manager at home.

The Operations Manager told the guard to get an updated loading plan from the flight follower. The revised plan from the flight follower showed how to load the cargo pallets into the 18 slots on the plane. Only two slots would be empty: slot 2 (near the front) and slot 13 (near the back). All the other slots would be filled.

The Aeromar crew loaded the first cargo pallet at 10:30 a.m., but the Operations Manager forgot to tell the crew to remove the 1,000 pounds.

After the crew had filled most of the plane from back to front, they discovered that the pallet for slot 5 (near the front) was too big to fit in a standard slot. To solve this problem, the crew pushed the other pallets backward, filling slot 13 near the back of the plane. This freed up space so the oversized pallet could use slot 5 and part of slot 4. When the cargo doors closed, the Aeromar loaders had filled the plane leaving slot 2 open, as was planned, and part of slot 4 open due to the oversized pallet. Slot 13 was full with a pallet, but it should have been empty, according to the Fine Air loading instructions. This oversight meant that more weight was near the back of the plane.

The loaders finished with the last pallet at 12:06 p.m.

The plane taxied to the runway at 12:32 p.m. The control tower cleared the flight for takeoff two minutes later. Shortly after takeoff, the nose of the plane pitched upwards. The plane entered an aerodynamic stall. The pilot could not regain control, and the plane came crashing into a parking lot near the airport. Five people died: four on the plane and one man in his car in the parking lot.

What went wrong?

The accident investigators found that the plane had pitched up due to the back of the plane being too heavy. In pilot-speak, the center of gravity was too far aft. The crew couldn't recover control of the plane after takeoff.

What caused this?

This accident was the result of a combination of process failures:

- The Aeromar Operations Manager failed to remove the 1,000 extra pounds from the plane.
- The flight follower failed to verify that the cargo loaders made the final weight distribution changes.
- The Aeromar cargo supervisor failed to load the pallets according to the approved load plan.
- Aeromar failed to keep pallets within size limitations. The one oversized pallet interfered with the loading plan.
- Fine Air failed to verify pallet weights and proper load distribution before takeoff.

And the National Transportation Safety Board's investigation turned up even more process problems. Fine Air did not calculate the plane's center of gravity properly. Aeromar did not have written instructions for how to load a plane: Aeromar cargo handlers said they received only verbal instructions about how to load an airplane when they were first assigned to the cargo ramp.[13]

Fine Air and Aeromar had many opportunities to spot and correct the errors that led to this accident. However, their unwillingness to improve their processes led to tragedy.

Ideas from Fine Air Flight 101

- Teach new team members the right way to do things, provide a written reference, and verify adherence to the correct process.
- Encourage anyone on the team to call a "time-out" if they see something that is not right.
- Create a checklist and don't skip items based on your assumptions.

Process failures on the USS Connecticut

The USS Connecticut is a U.S. Navy nuclear-powered, fast-attack submarine. During a routine mission in the South China Sea, the sub hit an undersea mountain. The accident led to the dismissal of the vessel's commanding officer, the executive officer, and the Chief of the Boat. A mishap like this leaves a stain on the records of those officers and could even lead to early retirement.

In a Navy press release, Vice Admiral Karl Thomas, the fleet commander, said that this incident could have been prevented by "sound judgment, prudent decision-making, and adherence to required procedures in navigation planning, watch team execution, and risk management."[14]

According to the admiral's statement, the submarine's leaders failed in one or more of these processes:

- How to plan the boat's navigation. Decide where the boat will go and when.
- How to lead a watch team. Assign responsibility for tracking where you are and what's around you.
- How to manage risk. Be aware of what could go wrong, including running into an underwater mountain.

Ideas from the USS Connecticut

- Remain vigilant and follow processes, even when everything is calm.
- Be aware of the possible obstacles and stick to a plan to avoid them.

Checklist for improving your processes by learning from others

☐ For stories about process success, ask, "What are the ways we can apply the discipline and tenacity displayed by these process leaders?"

☐ For stories about process failure, remember that hindsight is 20/20, and we might not have performed any better in these situations.

☐ Ask yourself, "What are the things I can do today to improve my processes, remove variation, and eliminate waste?"

☐ Ask yourself, "What can I change now to prepare for future events and avoid bad outcomes?"

☐ List the factors that affect how you make process decisions: time pressure, peer pressure, training you've received, your company culture, and your habits.

- Which of those factors could result in a bad decision?
- How can that be corrected?

Chapter 15

How to Improve Your Processes Using External Resources

Identify	Describe	Use	Improve
Chapter 4. Identify Your **Functional Areas**		Chapter 10. Use Your Processes in **Day-to-Day Work**	Chapter 13. **Improve** Your Processes
Chapter 5. Identify Your **Roles**	Chapter 8. Describe Your Processes With **Attributes**	Chapter 11. Use Your Processes With **Your Team**	Chapter 14. Improve Your Processes by **Learning from Others**
Chapter 6. Identify Your **Processes**	Chapter 9. Describe Your Processes Using **How-To Guides**	Chapter 12. Use Your Processes With **Business Frameworks**	Chapter 15. Improve Your Processes Using **External Resources**
Chapter 7. Identify **Gaps and Opportunities**			

Congratulations! You've seen how the Process Prescription works from start to finish. As we conclude this book, let's review some additional resources and suggestions for implementing the Process Prescription. Specifically, we'll look at templates, consulting, and software.

Since tools and resources are changing and improving, we'll look at some general principles for choosing the right resources instead of providing a checklist of specific "must-haves." This chapter covers how to choose additional resources in a vendor-neutral way without requiring a particular solution.

For more detailed information about specific vendors, providers, and solutions, visit the Process Prescription website. Scan the QR code below or visit ProcessPrescription.com.

Figure 15-1. Link to Resources. Scan this QR code for quick access to online resources.

You may also send an email to hello@processprescription.com to receive a list of resources.

Evaluating your process needs

The way you implement the Process Prescription will depend on your needs. Similarly, how you pick tools and resources will depend on your team, budget, industry, and other factors.

If you're just starting your Process Prescription journey, then your focus is on the "Identify" step. If you're well underway, you're probably more interested in the "Use" and "Improve" steps of the Process Prescription.

Let's look at the four main steps of the Process Prescription and typical needs based on where you are in this journey.

Step 1 - Identifying your processes

If you're at the Identify step of the Process Prescription, you may be considering options, researching, and figuring out what to do first.

To move forward, finish identifying your organization's functional areas and roles. If you have specific roadblocks or concerns, write those down and brainstorm ways to overcome them. You can also discuss your challenges with someone who has already begun applying the Process Prescription. Ask them how they solved the problems or uncertainty that you're facing.

You can team up with someone to journey through the Process Prescription together. Your partner could be someone in your own organization or someone in a different business who shares your commitment to process thinking. Compare notes and learn from each other. Copy each other's successes and avoid each other's failures. Hold each other accountable for making progress.

Step 2 - Describing your processes

At this step, you've begun to add attributes and create How-to Guides.

Don't think you need fancy new software to start creating How-to Guides and your Process Library. Use your existing software tools to make lists and describe processes. When you know your rhythm and preferences for using and updating your How-to Guides, consider new tools to make things faster and easier.

As Peter Drucker said, "Plans are only good intentions unless they immediately degenerate into hard work." Do something. Crack open a How-to Guide template and capture some of your process thoughts. Design and run an experiment to discover the best way to describe and use a process. If it works, repeat it. If it partly works, improve it. If it fails, try something else.

Step 3 - *Using your processes*

If you're at this stage with the Process Prescription, then you've document-ed some of your processes, and you're using them to complete tasks. You've overcome obstacles along the way, and you need to keep the momentum going. It's okay to take small steps as long as they're forward. Find out what's worked best as you've implemented the Process Prescription and trained people to replicate that success.

As you continue your process journey, work on the following to accelerate the benefits:

- Set a goal to increase the portion of your routine work that is described by a process.
- Quantify how you'll know when you've achieved your goal. You need clear criteria for success.
- Set a deadline to begin using processes with specific roles in your business.
- Generalize routines and make them into shareable templates.
- Continue to document your non-routine activities to get visibility into how they work and how to improve them.
- Refine your templates for creating new How-to Guides and processes.
- Optimize and integrate your current software tools.
- Assign who's doing what and when.
- Identify "process thinking" skills that would be most valuable for your team to acquire.

Step 4 - *Improving your processes*

At this stage, you're moving forward, and you're largely self-sufficient in your process journey. You're ready to tackle just about anything that comes at you. You've moved through the Identify, Describe, and Use steps. Now you're working on the Improve step. As part of your continuous process improvement, consider working on the following:

- Have an expert review your processes and provide feedback.

- Get help on a particular improvement initiative, especially if it involves software or equipment that requires specialized knowledge.
- Simplify processes by removing steps that don't directly add value.
- Automate repetitive processes.
- Apply analytical tools to find more things to improve.
- Fine-tune your software stack to make capturing and improving your processes easier.
- Identify limitations of your current software so you can request new features, find workarounds, fill gaps, or switch to a new application.

Getting the resources you need

Let's look at three types of resources that can help during your Process Prescription journey: templates, consultants, and software.

More ideas and tools are available at ProcessPrescription.com.

How to find and use templates

A template is a standard, reusable pattern that you can convert into a version that works for your particular situation. A template gives you a headstart on making something useful.

Templates include sample documents, blank forms, idea lists, topical outlines, checklists, worksheets, printable signs, standard messages, and sample inputs. In manufacturing, a template can be a physical object or example used to standardize production.

A template helps you complete a process step by giving you an example to follow. Multiple processes can use the same template. Create links in your How-to Guides to any related templates. Organize your templates for quick access using labels, template IDs, and folders.

A set of templates from the chapters in this book are available at ProcessPrescription.com. These include the verb list, noun list, a sample Process Matrix, and a How-to Guide template.

Modify a template to create your customized version. For example, when using the How-to Guide template, discard anything that doesn't apply to your organization. Remove, rearrange, and reformat sections until you have a layout that works best for you. As you use your processes and find patterns, create better templates.

Many of the process "nouns" we've looked at could benefit from a template. When you're creating something new (such as a document, product, or event), use a template to standardize your process and save time.

Here are some types of templates that I've found helpful:

- Email templates for marketing, surveys, newsletters, and notifications
- Budget planning worksheet
- Strategic Financial Plan template
- Trip planning template
- Marketing planning template
- Event planning template
- Proposal template
- Report template

How to find and use coaches and consultants

If your implementation of the Process Prescription is going smoothly, you may not need advice from outside your organization.

But who do you turn to if you need help? Or if you need help with improving one particular process? Or if you've gotten stuck on a step? Or if you want a second opinion about how to solve a process problem?

A medical doctor answers health questions. A Certified Public Accountant answers accounting questions. But where do you find a process doctor, process therapist, or process coach?

The website ProcessPrescription.com provides some ideas for finding help. Once you've identified someone who could help, take a few more steps to ensure they're a good fit before inviting them to work with you.

Understand a consultant's bias

There are many types of process consultants who specialize in particular functional areas, certain industries, or specific technologies. There's no standard consultant profile or certification that guarantees that someone will be of help to you. *Caveat emptor.*

To evaluate a potential consultant, understand their background and approach. Every consultant has a bias or perspective from which they view the world. This includes how they view business challenges and how they devise solutions. A technology consultant thinks in terms of applications and data. An accountant thinks about financial implications and compliance. A lawyer can foresee risks and potential problems related to agreements. While these experts can provide useful insights, also realize the limitations of specialist consultant. Don't allow them to divert your attention toward a topic that's valuable for them but a distraction for you.

Warren Buffett once said, "Never ask your barber if you need a haircut." Similarly, never ask a software reseller if you need what they're selling. Of course, you need their software!

For example, management consultants who bill by the hour (or by the project) want a way to keep the work flowing and the revenue recurring. I know a consulting firm that urges its consultants to always be on the lookout for new projects, so they can continue to bill the client. I'm not suggesting impropriety here; finding new ways to create value for clients is smart consulting. If you're paying for the consulting, you need to understand the consultant's preferences and underlying motivations.

Find out what else the consultant sells

Some consultants sell a product that complements their consulting business. Learn about all of a consultant's revenue sources before you hire them. Ask what percentage of their revenue comes from various sources. Expect to be offered their other products and services. This "one stop shopping" can be convenient if you need what they offer. But before buying extra services, consider if the service really fits your need, if the price is competitive, and if another vendor provides a better alternative.

Add-on products and services offered by consultants include off-the-shelf software, custom software development, training, business process outsourcing, and fractional CxO services.

Define what you want the consultant to do

Before a consultant begins work, you both need to agree to a written work plan with well-defined tasks and deliverables.

In software development, the acronym CRUD describes four basic ways applications work with data: Create, Read, Update, and Delete. We can also use CRUD to define the basic ways that a consultant can help improve your processes.

- Create. The consultant creates a new process for you to use.
- Read. The consultant reads (and follows) process documentation to complete tasks for you.
- Update. The consultant helps you improve an existing process.
- Delete. The consultant helps you eliminate waste through automation or simplification.

Match the consultant's work to your specific processes that they are helping to improve. If you can't make the match, don't waste your money.

If a consultant develops a new process that you want to run in-house eventually, learn as much as you can about the process from the consultant, or have the consultant teach you how to run the process. If you're okay with the consultant continuing to run the process for you as a service, then focus on providing everything they need when they need it. Make it easy for them to run the process and add value to your business.

You also need to define who owns the intellectual property generated from the consultant's work. Is the work product exclusively yours, exclusively theirs, or shared?

After establishing a high level of trust, collaborate with your consultant and ask them, "What other processes can you help us create or improve?"

When implementing the Process Prescription, a consultant could help you with the following tasks:

- Identify your processes

- ◦ Identify functional areas and subareas
- ◦ Create and refine a role-based org chart
- ◦ Identify existing and needed processes
- Describe your processes
  - ◦ Develop an interview guide for conducting role interviews
  - ◦ Assign process owners, process schedules, and process priorities
  - ◦ Create a How-to Guide template for your organization
  - ◦ Create labels for categorizing processes and finding patterns
- Use your processes
  - ◦ Create a Process Library and document hierarchy
  - ◦ Set up software for process management or knowledge management
  - ◦ Conduct individualized coaching
  - ◦ Evaluate opportunities for outsourcing
- Improve your processes
  - ◦ Provide training on process thinking and process improvement
  - ◦ Optimize your existing software for process improvement
  - ◦ Identify technology or tools to fill gaps and accelerate process improvement
  - ◦ Find opportunities for simplification, waste reduction, and automation
  - ◦ Prioritize improvement opportunities
  - ◦ Build a culture that includes process thinking

Start with a small project

Can you identify a starter project for the consultant? Instead of creating a project with a large batch of tasks, pick something with high value, clear deliverables, and a reasonable cost.

Starting small reduces your risk and the inertia required to get things rolling. You'll spend less time defining the project and see results faster.

If the consultant meets your expectations on the starter project, expand the relationship to include more tasks and deliverables. If the consultant only works on an "all or nothing" basis and requires a hefty financial commitment upfront, then look elsewhere for help.

How to find and use the right software

Implementing the Process Prescription does not require expensive software. You can use your existing software to get started, then evaluate more specialized tools as you continue your process journey.

Consider the two broad types of software that your organization already uses:

- Vertical, specialized software that focuses on your industry or a specific functional area.
- Horizontal, general software that works across your organization to facilitate productivity and collaboration.

Ensure that your horizontal software works with your core, vertical systems by sharing data, documents, and messages. Treat your core system as your hub, and then connect other applications to the hub. Avoid creating a mishmash of fragmented applications that don't talk to each other. Your objective should be to develop a cohesive software portfolio that combines vertical specialized tools and horizontal process tools.

Maximize your vertical software first

Vertical software works within one functional area or one industry, such as the following:

- Payroll software (within the Finance function)
- Applicant tracking software (with the Human Resources function)
- Shipping software (with the Product Delivery function)
- Advertising software (within the Marketing function)

If you're using a core, vertical application that works well, continue to invest in learning and using that. If you need additional features beyond your core software's capabilities, ask the software vendor to add the new features you need. Find add-ons that provide the extra features you need. Visit the "Integrations" page on the software vendor's website to find complementary solutions or ask them what other software they would recommend to fill the gaps.

If your core software is not meeting your needs, if it's not being upgraded fast enough by the vendor, or if it can't integrate with other solutions, then it may be time to replace your core software. This software surgery typically requires significant effort to convert your existing data and train everyone on the new system. With a careful migration plan, switching to a new core system can give you a fresh start and a new platform to build a leaner, faster, process-focused business.

Standardize your horizontal software

Horizontal software works across multiple functional areas, spanning all columns of the Process Matrix. Examples include the following:

- Collaboration & Messaging: email, messaging, video, scheduling
- Productivity software: documents, notes, spreadsheets, presentations, drawings
- Process Management
- Customer Relationship Management
- Knowledge Management

Horizontal software is important since it touches every functional area of your business. Choose either a software suite or a "best in class" collection of integrated tools, then standardize on using this horizontal toolset across your organization. Avoid using overlapping solutions since it's wasteful. Here are some examples of overlapping software that I've seen in the same organization.

- Two video conferencing solutions
- Three ways to create notes and documentation
- Two apps for creating video content
- Two apps for creating spreadsheets
- Two ways of sharing files
- Two form-builder tools

- Two ways to send chat messages
- Two methods for scheduling meetings

Redundancy like that wastes time and money. People have to figure out which tool to use, where to store things, and where to find things. Also, there's the extra cost of software licensing, maintenance, and training. If you have two applications that do nearly the same thing, pick a winner and migrate everyone to the single solution.

Some overlap among your applications will happen as you add new technology, but it gets chaotic if everyone picks their favorite software without standardization.

Know what you want process management software to do

Process management software falls in the "horizontal" category since it helps you organize, categorize, document, and improve processes across all your functional areas.

Your process management software should increase clarity, collaboration, and consistency. Based on the Process Prescription's four main steps, here are some things to expect from your process management software:

Identify processes
- Catalog all your processes, not just a few of them.
- Categorize processes by functional area and subarea.
- Capture the roles in your business and the related processes.
- Assign people to each role.

Describe processes
- Capture "who's doing what and when" for your organization.
- Create a Process Library, which serves as a single place to find, filter, prioritize, and update your processes.
- Assign roles to each process.
- Link resources to each process. Resources include How-to Guides, templates, related files, applications, and tools.
- Schedule processes to generate and track recurring tasks.

Use processes
- Send reminders automatically for upcoming, scheduled processes.
- Access, follow, and refine your How-to Guides for each process.

- See the status of assigned tasks.
- Integrate your existing documents and resources to create a unified view of your processes.

Improve processes
- Label, filter, and prioritize processes.
- Apply analytical tools to find quick fixes and top opportunities.
- Find and group processes that can be improved using a particular tool or technique.

Checklist for improving your processes using external resources

☐ Assess your resource needs based on the Process Prescription step (Identify, Describe, Use, Improve) you're working on. Don't skip a step and do a deep dive into one area without getting an overview of all your processes.

☐ Use templates when creating How-to Guides and checklists. Modify templates to meet your organization's needs.

☐ Identify a consultant's bias and the extra products that they sell.

☐ When working with a consultant, agree on clear tasks and deliverables.

☐ Evaluate your software applications based on the processes that they support. Maximize your core tools, then add new capabilities.

The Path Forward

Now that you've seen the Process Prescription from start-to-finish, you're ready to spot new opportunities based on problems you encounter.

You're ready to combine long-term, strategic thinking with the essential, day-to-day details of running your business.

You're ready to help people understand and improve the way they work.

You're ready to apply lean thinking to simplify and streamline.

You're ready to work on your business in ways that deliver more fulfillment and more value.

I wish you the best in your process success!

References

Chapter 1

1. *Lemonade Insurance Company.* Demotech. (2022, November 17). https://www.demotech.com/company/16023
2. James, M., Kaufman, A., & Wick, J. (2022, April 15). The day Alec Baldwin shot Halyna Hutchins and Joel Souza. *Los Angeles Times.* https://www.latimes.com/entertainment-arts/business/story/2021-10-31/rust-film-alec-baldwin-shooting-what-happened-that-day
3. Lee, A., & Lee, W. (2021, October 24). Lack of movie prop gun safety led to Alec Baldwin shooting. *Los Angeles Times.* https://www.latimes.com/entertainment-arts/movies/story/2021-10-22/rust-shooting-movie-prop-gun-safety-blanks-rounds-more
4. *Proverbs 14:23 (NIV).* (n.d.). Bible Gateway. https://www.bible-gateway.com/passage/?search=Proverbs+14:23

5. Air Safety Institute. (2016, August 24). *Accident Case Study: Unintended Consequences* [Video]. YouTube. https://www.youtube.com/watch?v=BXr3xr4rj98

6. UpFlip. (2021, January 18). *KAIZEN: Change Your Business and Create Success (with Paul Akers) Pt. 1.* YouTube. https://www.youtube.com/watch?v=Zah9panf7ag

7. Paul Akers. (2021, March 27). *You Can't Teach Lean!* [Video]. YouTube. https://www.youtube.com/watch?v=p5eDG9UyqAA

Chapter 2

1. Drucker, P. F. (1986). *Managing for Results* (First Perennial Library Edition). (p. 117) Harper Collins.

2. Gerber, M. E. (2001). *The E-Myth Revisited: Why Most Small Businesses Don't Work and What to Do About It* (p. 97). Harper Business.

3. Ibid, p. 104

4. Carpenter, S. (2011). *Work the System: The Simple Mechanics of Making More and Working Less.* (p. 9). Greenleaf Book Group.

5. Wickman, G. (2012). *Traction: Get a Grip on Your Business (Expanded ed.).* (p. 152). BenBella Books.

6. Mentour Pilot. (2021, August 13). *Easyjet A320 tells United Boeing 787 to GO AROUND! | Serious Aircraft Incident* [Video]. YouTube. https://www.youtube.com/watch?v=AM01NSZyA7I

7. *Never Events | PSNet.* (2019, September 8). https://psnet.ahrq.gov/primer/never-events

8. Zwilling, M. (2021, January 15). 7 reasons to prioritize attention to your team ahead of procedure. *Inc.com.* https://www.inc.com/martin-zwilling/7-reasons-to-prioritize-attention-to-your-team-ahead-of-procedure.html

9. Smith, T. (2015, November 3). 5 things people who love their jobs have in common. *FastCompany.com.* https://www.fastcompany.com/3052985/5-things-people-who-love-their-jobs-have-in-common

Chapter 4

1. *Short-Term Memory: Up to 7 Items, But Highly Volatile.* (n.d.). https://thebrain.mcgill.ca/flash/capsules/experience_jaune03.html
2. *1 Chronicles 27:25-34 (NKJV).* (n.d.). Bible Gateway. https://www.biblegateway.com/passage/?search=1+Chronicles+27:25-34

Chapter 6

1. *1 Corinthians 12:20-22 (NASB1995).* (n.d.). Bible Gateway. https://www.biblegateway.com/passage/?search=1+Corinthians+12:20-22
2. TRW Systems. (1971). *PGNS/AGS Summary Card.* Manned Spacecraft Center / National Aeronautics and Space Administration. http://pid.emory.edu/ark:/25593/spfsp

Chapter 9

1. The Contradictions That Drive Toyota's Success. (2014, August 1). *Harvard Business Review.* https://hbr.org/2008/06/the-contradictions-that-drive-toyotas-success
2. Ratcliffe, S. (2011). *Concise Oxford Dictionary of Quotations (Oxford Quick Reference) (6th ed.).* (p. 389). Oxford University Press.
3. Svoboda, M. (n.d.). *The expert at anything was once a beginner.* Quotepark.com. https://quotepark.com/quotes/1067036-helen-hayes-the-expert-at-anything-was-once-a-beginner/

Chapter 10

1. Dan Martell. (2017, June 19). *How To Create a Business Playbook: How To Make SOPs* [Video]. YouTube. https://youtube.com/watch?v=cfsH5rjcaW8
2. Maslow, A. (1966). *The Psychology of Science: A Reconnaissance.* (p. 15). HarperCollins.
3. Calabrese G. J. (2013). Pitching mechanics, revisited. *International journal of sports physical therapy*, 8(5), (pp. 652—660).

Chapter 11

1. Schwantes, M. (2018, December 3). Warren Buffett says if you hire people on intelligence but they lack... *Inc.com*. https://www.inc-com/marcel-schwantes/warren-buffet-says-you-should-hire-people-based-on-these-3-traits-but-only-1-truly-matters.html

2. *Edison's Lightbulb*. (2017, May 19). The Franklin Institute. https://www.fi.edu/history-resources/edisons-lightbulb

Chapter 12

1. Harnish, V. (2002). *Mastering the Rockefeller Habits: What You Must Do to Increase the Value of Your Growing Firm*. Gazelles, Inc.

2. Senge, P. M. (2006). *The Fifth Discipline: The Art & Practice of the Learning Organization*. Currency.

3. Building a Learning Organization. (1993. July-August). *Harvard Business Review*. https://hbr.org/1993/07/building-a-learning-organization

4. Wickman, G. (2012). *Traction: Get a Grip on Your Business (Expanded ed.)*. BenBella Books.

5. Gerber, M. E. (2001). *The E-Myth Revisited: Why Most Small Businesses Don't Work and What to Do About It*. Harper Business.

6. Marcus Lemonis. (2021, January 29). *3 Key To Business Success: People, Process & Product*. https://www.marcuslemonis.com/business/3ps-of-business

7. *Enduring Ideas: The 7-S Framework*. (2018, February 9). McKinsey & Company. https://www.mckinsey.com/capabilities/strategy-and-corporate-finance/our-insights/enduring-ideas-the-7-s-framework

8. Carpenter, S. (2011). *Work the System: The Simple Mechanics of Making More and Working Less*. Greenleaf Book Group.

9. Akers, P. A. (2014). *2 Second Lean 3rd Edition*. FastCap LLC.

10. Doerr, J., & Page, L. (2018). *Measure What Matters: How Google, Bono, and the Gates Foundation Rock the World with OKRs*. Van Haren Publishing.

Chapter 13

1. Gaille, B. (2017, January 13). *13 Invaluable Shigeo Shingo Quotes.* BrandonGaille.com. https://brandongaille.com/13-invaluable-shigeo-shingo-quotes/

2. *Washington's Mickles in a Pickle.* (n.d.). https://boston1775.blogspot.com/2016/06/washingtons-mickles-in-pickle.html

3. Texas A&M Athletics. (2021, October 10). *Alabama Postgame: Jimbo Fisher* [Video]. YouTube. https://www.youtube.com/watch?v=ykIYwnHA6U4

4. Wikipedia contributors. (2022, September 17). *Taiichi Ohno.* Wikipedia. https://en.wikipedia.org/wiki/Taiichi_Ohno

5. Paul Akers. (2022, May 28). *AME Tour 14 Gangster Lean* [Video]. YouTube. https://www.youtube.com/watch?v=pQNtoO9IQ4U

6. *Drywall Finish Levels Explained.* (2022, June 29). The Spruce. https://www.thespruce.com/the-five-levels-of-drywall-finishing-4120152

7. *Lean Thinking and Methods - 5S.* (2022, October 31). US EPA. https://www.epa.gov/sustainability/lean-thinking-and-methods-5s

8. Musk, E. [@elonmusk]. Elon Musk on.* (2018, April 13). Yes, excessive automation at Tesla was a mistake. To be precise, my mistake. Humans are underrated. [Tweet] Retrieved from https://twitter.com/elonmusk/status/984882630947753984

9. *Patient Safety: Use "Time Outs" to Re-Establish Focus and Eliminate Medical Errors.* (2017, September 12). Stanford Health Care. https://stanfordhealthcare.org/health-care-professionals/medical-staff/medstaff-update/2014-february/201402-patient-safety.html

10. Wroblewski, M. (2009, April 29). *'Get your boots on!': Toyota's spin on genchi genbutsu.* Reliable Plant. https://www.reliableplant.com/Read/17263/%E2%80%98get-your-boots-on!%E2%80%99-toyota%E2%80%99s-spin-on-genchi-genbutsu

11. *Shingo's 10 Wasted Years.* (2020, October 14). Paul Akers Website. https://paulakers.net/2020/lean-videos/shingos-10-wasted-years

Chapter 14

1. Supreme Lending Southeast. (2021, August 24). *Nick Saban: The Process* [Video]. YouTube. https://www.youtube.com/watch?v=XEgBu1pfTi4

2. Boisvert, Z. (Ed.). (n.d.). Saban Notes. Coach Jackson Pages. http://coachjacksonspages.com/Sabannotes.pdf

3. Boisvert, Z. (Ed.). (n.d.). Saban Notes. Coach Jackson Pages. http://coachjacksonspages.com/Sabannotes.pdf

4. Texas A&M Athletics. (2021, October 10). *Alabama Postgame: Jimbo Fisher* [Video]. YouTube. https://www.youtube.com/watch?v=ykIYwnHA6U4

5. Brown, A. (Director). (2020, March 12). *The Test* (season 1, episode 1). Amazon Prime Video.

6. *Enduring Ideas: Portfolio of initiatives.* (2018, February 9). McKinsey & Company. https://www.mckinsey.com/capabilities/strategy-and-corporate-finance/our-insights/enduring-ideas-portfolio-of-initiatives

7. Court, D., Elzinga, D., Mulder, S., & Vetvik, O. J. (2021, March 31). *The consumer decision journey.* McKinsey & Company. https://www.mckinsey.com/capabilities/growth-marketing-and-sales/our-insights/the-consumer-decision-journey

8. *Enduring Ideas: The three horizons of growth.* (2022, August 25). McKinsey & Company. https://www.mckinsey.com/capabilities/strategy-and-corporate-finance/our-insights/enduring-ideas-the-three-horizons-of-growth

9. *Walters & Wolf.* (n.d.). [Video]. YouTube. https://www.youtube.com/channel/UCFyGskstcUF-yknIermcgzA

10. The Boeing Company (2009). *777 Quick Reference Handbook.* Qatar Airways. http://www.737ng.co.uk/B777%20QRH%20Quick%20reference%20Handbook.pdf

11. Vital Signs: Central Line—Associated Blood Stream Infections—United States, 2001, 2008, and 2009. (2011). In *Morbidity and Mortality Weekly Report (MMWR)*. Centers for Disease Control and Prevention. https://www.cdc.gov/mmwr/preview/mmwrhtml/mm6008a4.htm#:~:text=In%202001%2C%20the%20pooled%20mean,%2Ddays%20(Table%201).

12. Gawande, A. (2011). *The Checklist Manifesto: How to Get Things Right* (First). Picador.

13. National Transportation Safety Board. (1998). *Uncontrolled Impact With Terrain Fine Airlines Flight 101* (No. PB98-910402). https://www.ntsb.gov/investigations/AccidentReports/Reports/AAR9802.pdf

14. U.S. Navy Office of Information. (2021, November 4). *USS Connecticut (SSN 22) Command Leadership Relief* [Press release]. https://www.navy.mil/Press-Office/Press-Releases/display-pressreleases/Article/2833857/uss-connecticut-ssn-22-command-leadership-relief/

Index of Figures

Index of Topics, by category

This index lists topics alphabetically within seven categories: Business Types, Companies & Organizations, Concepts & Tools, Functions & Departments, People, Roles & Titles, and Software.

254

Companies & Organizations

Concepts & Tools

Roles & Titles

Index of How-to Topics

You can adapt some of these into full-fledged How-to Guides by adding details and instructions based on your organization's needs.

For additional tools and resources, visit ProcessPrescription.com

www.ingramcontent.com/pod-product-compliance
Lightning Source LLC
Chambersburg PA
CBHW071551210326
41597CB00019B/3202